MW01291246

Answering The Call

Answering The Call

The Story Of Grace On Wings,
The Nation's Only Charity Air Ambulance

James R. Milstead, M.D.

For permission to use material, schedule a flight, or arrange for a guest speaker, contact:

James R. Milstead, M.D.
P.O. Box 455
Plainfield, IN 46168
877-754-7223
Email jim.milstead@graceonwings.org

All proceeds from the sale of this book go directly to the ministry of Grace on Wings, Inc.

This book is dedicated to all of our volunteers who sacrifice their time, talents, and treasures for the benefit of those we serve. Thank you for showing the love of Christ to the world!

Contents

Foreword xi
Preface.. xiii
Acknowledgments...xvii

1 My Plans For You
   ("I'm Not Quite Dead Yet").................................. 19

2 A Prodigal Son Returns
   ("The Wandering Jew") 30

3 Lean Not On Your Own Wisdom
   ("Me, A Doctor? Didn't See That Coming!")......... 40

4 Stepping Out In Faith
   ("You Want Me To Go Where?")......................... 49

5 Crisis Of Belief
   ("Hal Must Be Crazy!").................................... 59

6 Attempt Great Things For God
   ("You Need How Much?") 68

7 Experiencing God's Blessings
   ("Whoa, Nellie!") 79

8 Leaving A Legacy
   ("The Gift That Keeps On Giving") 87

9 Knowing And Serving God Better
("An Invitation To The Feast") 95

10 Following His Lead
("Here, There, And Everywhere") 104

11 All Things Through Christ
("Heart Of A Lion") 110

12 Parting The Seas
("Houston, We Have A Problem") 121

13 Trusting The Lord To Provide
("Well, Sort Of") 130

14 Sheltered From The Storm
("Life Is Like A ...") 140

15 Boast Only In The Lord
("I'm A Humble Guy—Oops!") 151

16 Abiding In The Vine
("Branching Out, But Not On Your Own") 160

Testimonials 167
Notes 173

Foreword

*A*nswering the Call tells a wonderful and yet unlikely success story. It tells the story of a group of people who were called to provide services that no one ever hopes to use: emergency medical services and medical transport services. It tells the story of Grace on Wings, a nonprofit, fixed-wing air medical transport company based in Indianapolis, Indiana.

Air medical services have become an integral component of modern healthcare systems, and Grace on Wings, like all their ground medical transport and air medical transport colleagues, strives to provide the highest quality medical care and safest, most effective air medical transportation to patients in need. Like their colleagues, Grace on Wings provides life-saving medical care to fellow human beings in their most vulnerable moments. What makes Grace on Wings different is their services are based on a Christian mission statement, "Showing Christ's Love Through Aviation."

Answering the Call is the inspirational story of a group of people from very different backgrounds and with very different interests and skills who have come together to serve their fellow men and women when they most need that help and assistance. They seek neither recognition nor personal gain from their services and believe they have been brought together by God to be instruments of his help and assistance in our world. What makes *Answering the Call* an unlikely success story is that it works!

Grace on Wings developed as an idea—without any facilities, without any aircraft, without any financial backing, and without a dedicated team—by people who were called to make it work. Today,

Grace on Wings has flown patients for nearly six years. They have been recognized by their peers, receiving the Association of Air Medical Service's Fixed Wing Award of Excellence at the 2012 Air Medical Transport Conference.

Answering the Call tells the story of people of faith who were called to serve others and who believed God would provide them with the challenges, opportunities, and resources to serve him by serving their fellow human beings in need. At every point in their journey to create Grace on Wings, they were challenged to place their faith in God and believe seemingly impossible tasks were actually possible because God was calling them to take that journey. The statement "this is just crazy without God being involved" was made by a board member at Grace on Wing's first board meeting, and it has been applicable many times throughout their journey.

Answering the Call is an incredible story of service and faith. It will touch your heart and inspire you to serve others in need.

Rick Sherlock
President & CEO,
Association of Air Medical Services &
The MedEvac Foundation International

Preface

The first time I seriously considered writing a book about Grace on Wings was at the 2011 Air Medical Transport Conference (AMTC) in St. Louis. A physician from the Cleveland Clinic had heard about our ministry, and he sought me out to thank me for the work we were doing. "You need to write a book to inspire others to volunteer like you guys do," he said.

That seed germinated in my mind over the next year. When Grace on Wings received an award at the 2012 AMTC in Seattle for being the best fixed-wing air ambulance service, I knew the time had come.

So why did I write this book? First, I want to share the story of Grace on Wings in the hope others will be inspired to attempt great things for God by hearing how he is working in and through Grace on Wings for his glory. Second, I hope to increase the awareness of our ministry so more patients will be able to be served. Many people, even in Indianapolis, still have never heard of Grace on Wings. Third, I hope to attract more volunteers and donors to grow the ministry for many years to come. And last, I want to chronicle the major events of the formation and evolution of the ministry for history's sake.

As you will discover as you read, Grace on Wings is made up of a lot of ordinary people doing extraordinary things because we are called by God to do so. It's as simple or as complicated as that. Do we make mistakes? Certainly. Do we worry when the finances are tight or the flight requests are scarce? You bet. But we are continually amazed at the way God provides for all our needs in spite of our shortcomings. This book tells how God has worked throughout our lives to bring us to the point where he could use us to serve others.

I am an ER doctor, not a theologian, a pastor, or a professional writer. Late one night as I was trying to decide on appropriate titles to capture the message of each chapter, I became a little giddy. I wrote an "alternative" title for each one. I decided to keep both titles, thinking some readers might better relate to the alternatives than the formal titles.

The patients' stories woven into the chapters are real and were chosen to illustrate how God is at work in the lives of his people, in times of challenge and especially in times of personal tragedy. Many more could have been told. Every patient we have served has blessed us, as have their families and their loved ones. Thanks to each of you for giving us the privilege of sharing a part of your lives with us.

Before I began writing, I met with Donna Thomas to seek her wisdom and advice on how to proceed. Her book, *Climb Another Mountain*, was what had inspired me to take on this project. I told her of my ambition to write the story about Grace on Wings, but then quickly I confided I wasn't sure I was the right person for the job.

Cutting right to the heart of the matter in a way only Donna can, she simply asked, "Do you feel God has called you to write this book?"

Knowing at that moment I was questioning my calling from God while I would soon be urging others to be obedient to God's calling in their lives, I was convicted immediately. I realized the most important reason for writing this book was to be obedient to the call God had given me to do so.

"Yes" was my answer to Donna.

"So what is your question then?" she said.

As one well-known comedian would say, "Here's your sign!"

Should you attempt something great for God? Absolutely! Do not hesitate when God calls you to action. His timing is the one to follow, not your own. And remember, God will not give you an assignment he has not equipped you for, even though it may require a step of faith to believe it.

So here is my charge to everyone who reads this book: When you feel God calling you to join him in his work, don't miss the opportunity. The blessings you will receive and give to others, by answering the call, will far exceed your wildest dreams!

Acknowledgments

First and foremost, I want to thank all of the Grace on Wings volunteers who make this ministry possible. The pilots, nurses, paramedics, respiratory therapists, flight followers, and others who sacrifice their time to serve patients in need are the heart and soul of the organization.

Special thanks to the patients and families who shared their testimonies of how their lives were impacted by the ministry of Grace on Wings.

I am indebted to Donna Thomas for being my "Barnabas," my constant source of encouragement throughout this project. Your mentorship was invaluable.

This book could not have been written without the exceptional work of my editor, Karen Roberts. Thank you for your patience and professionalism in guiding me through this endeavor.

I am deeply grateful to everyone at Xulon Press for the wonderful work in getting this book published.

Most of all, I want to thank my wife for her encouragement, patience, and unconditional love.

1

My Plans For You
("I'm Not Quite Dead Yet!")

From my forward-facing seat in the cabin just aft of the cockpit, I watched the familiar ballet of flight unfold. As a former Air Force crewmember, I knew the drill well. Now, as Medical Director for Grace on Wings, my anxiety level was on the rise once again. Questions pelted my consciousness like hail pounding the windshield during a furious storm.

How long would our first mission take? Would the ground ambulance be there to meet us as planned when we arrived? And most importantly, in what condition would our patient be?

Watching Grace on Wings Chief Pilot and Founder, Hal Blank, at work in the cockpit was like witnessing a conductor orchestrating a symphony in the creation of heavenly music. Hal was not just a pilot—he was an aviator. He flew by instinct and feel, as though the plane were an extension of his very being.

I had seen his kind before, a breed of fearless and highly trained military pilots, during my time in the Air Force some forty years ago while traversing the unfriendly skies over Vietnam as a B-52 tail gunner. Hal's God-given talents were rare.

Cruising along in our MU-2 aircraft at three hundred miles an hour at an altitude of 18,000 feet above the planet, Hal was in his element. Glancing over his right shoulder, he said to me, "Jim, this is the best office in the world!"

Even after more than four thousand hours of piloting military and civilian aircraft, the liberating feeling Hal experienced during flight was as evident as ever. I could sense the peace that consumed him as he was freed for a while from the mundane daily activities on the earth far below.

From his perch in the left seat of the cockpit of the MU-2, the sleek workhorse plane designed by Mitsubishi nearly a half century before, Hal surveyed the brilliant, clear blue skies above and the dense, gray cloud deck several thousand feet below. I watched as he performed a station check of the aircraft's instrument panel. All systems were functioning in normal operating range as the plane sped southeast toward Miami, Florida, from Indianapolis, Indiana.

"Medevac 910 November Foxtrot, contact Atlanta center on 133.6," said the Indianapolis airspace controller.

"Roger Indianapolis. Medevac 910 November Foxtrot contacting Atlanta center on 133.6. Thank you, sir. God bless, and have a good day," Hal replied.

Young copilot Adam reached reflexively for the communication panel to dial in the new radio frequency, only to discover Hal already had tweaked in the required settings.

"We're finally on our way," Hal's wife Tami said over the intercom. Tami, Mission Coordinator and Co-founder of Grace on Wings, was seated in a crew position adjacent to the customized stretcher firmly attached to the right sidewall of the cabin. Her exclamation fractured the momentary silence.

Hal glanced back at Tami, and I could see a familiar look in his eyes. I suspected the competing emotions he had shared with me just before takeoff were on his mind.

Hal, I knew, was elated to accomplish the first mission of our fledgling organization. Nearly fifteen months after receiving a vision from the Lord to start the only faith-based charity air ambulance service in the United States, he was finally doing what he had been called to do — show the love of Christ through aviation. However, he was already being stretched beyond the scope of the organization's initial parameters.

Turning to look over his right shoulder, Hal said to the crew, "I never thought we would fly outside a five hundred mile radius from Indianapolis, and here we are going nearly a thousand miles to pick up our first patient!"

Hal had meticulously planned for this mission, as was his custom before any flight. He'd already factored in the unexpected distance. His many years of experience told him contingencies would arise when he least expected them, and he was determined to anticipate and overcome any obstacles he might encounter during this maiden voyage.

"We'll be starting our descent into the Ft. Lauderdale airport in just a few minutes," Hal said to the crew on the intercom. "Let's hope there's an ambulance to meet us so we can go get the patient."

His next comment was to Tami. "What's his name again, honey?"

"His name is Carlos. Carlos Escobar."

First Patient

The medical records I reviewed described Carlos Escobar as a healthy, 56-year-old man living in the Miami area prior to the time he became ill in June of 2007. A native of Guatemala, Carlos came to the United States in 1971 at age twenty. He attended Indiana University, where he obtained a degree in social work. Carlos also married during this time. In 1979, he and his wife moved to Florida, where he had worked as a social worker for many years. Later in his professional career, he performed administrative and teaching duties for the state of Florida.

Carlos first sought medical treatment for pain on the left side of his chest after something fell and struck him while he was working in his home. His doctor diagnosed him with a contusion and recommended that he take over-the-counter pain relievers. Some time later, Carlos developed a fever. No source of infection was found despite extensive testing during a two-week hospitalization.

Even with pain relievers and muscle relaxers, Carlos continued to have debilitating back and rib pain. Then, sometime in August or September of 2007, he developed weakness and spasticity of his lower extremities and lost all control of his bladder. An MRI revealed an epidural abscess along his spinal cord in the thoracic region.

Multiple surgeries, IV antibiotics, and a prolonged hospital stay failed to cure the infection. Carlos was left paralyzed below the level of his chest, bedridden in a Miami hospital, and seemingly without hope. His son, a member of the United States Marine Corps recently returned from military duty in Iraq, carried out an endless vigil at his father's bedside. He prayed continually for a miracle.

Carlos' youngest brother was a staff neonatologist and Director of Medical Genetics at St. Vincent Hospital in Indianapolis. I first learned of Carlos' condition when his brother told me he desperately wanted to transport Carlos to Indianapolis for surgery by his friend and colleague, a renowned spine surgeon. The surgeon said he would be happy to take care of Carlos if he could be transported to Indianapolis. Carlos' condition, however, would not allow him to be transported by commercial airliner because he could not sit up and required constant nursing care.

Carlos' brother had contemplated placing a mattress on the floor of a van and driving Carlos to Indianapolis himself. But ground transportation would be extremely long and arduous. The only available option, it seemed, was to fly Carlos from Ft. Lauderdale to Indianapolis by commercial air ambulance.

Carlos and his family were shocked to learn a typical air ambulance flight could cost anywhere from $20,000 to $100,000, depending on the services provided for the patient and the distance of the transport. Additionally, most insurance companies did not cover the cost of an air ambulance. Lacking the necessary finances, it seemed Carlos had no way of being transported safely from Miami to Indianapolis to obtain the life-saving medical care he so desperately needed. Carlos and his family fervently prayed for a miracle, and God answered their prayers in an unanticipated way.

First Test Of Faith

On Thanksgiving morning, November 22, 2007, Carlos' brother went to his mailbox and casually retrieved the daily newspaper. As he perused the front page of the *Indianapolis Star*, he was drawn to a lead article announcing the birth of a new charity air ambulance service called Grace on Wings. The paper said it was based in Indianapolis and served patients too ill for commercial flight or long-distance ground transport.

He read the article intently and felt a glimmer of hope. God had indeed heard his family's prayers, and maybe he was leading them to Grace on Wings to bring Carlos to Indianapolis.

He called the telephone number listed in the newspaper article and spoke with Hal. He explained the situation and received assurance that Carlos' situation was exactly the kind of mission for which Grace on Wings was created. After further discussion, Hal said he would have Tami begin the arrangements to bring Carlos to Indianapolis. The first mission of Grace on Wings was set in motion.

With some trepidation, Hal hung up the receiver and talked with Tami. Would the volunteer flight and medical personnel of the newly formed ministry be able to serve this gravely ill man without causing further harm to his fragile body? Would the distance of the flight be an issue? It was time to put faith into action.

Tami had been trained as a physical therapist and a physician assistant. When Grace on Wings was established, she was working as a physician assistant in orthopedics and in an ER setting. Her role in the new organization was as volunteer Mission Coordinator.

It was Tami's job to communicate with hospital social workers, medical personnel, patients, and their families to obtain the information necessary for Grace on Wings to accomplish a safe transfer of a patient in the most cost-effective manner. Also, Tami had to call nurses, paramedics, and respiratory therapists from the ministry's list of volunteers to assemble a medical crew tailored to the needs of the patient.

For this first mission on November 28, 2007, the medical crew Tami assembled consisted of a volunteer paramedic, physician assistant Tami Blank, and me, Dr. Jim Milstead, the medical doctor for the transport. The flight crew was made up of pilot Hal Blank and copilot Adam. All of us were eager to use our God-given talents to show the love of Christ to Carlos, his family, the medical staff at the hospital in Florida, and everyone we encountered along the way.

No mission of Grace on Wings would ever be undertaken without prayer covering. In response to the mission alert Hal sent by email, many Grace on Wings supporters had committed to pray for us as well as Carlos throughout the long journey.

First Transport

As we landed in Ft. Lauderdale, the sky was a deep shade of blue, laced with fluffy white clouds and illuminated by intense sunlight. When the entrance door located on the left rear side of the aircraft was opened, oppressive heat instantly enveloped us. It was a stark contrast to the steel gray sky and frigid temperatures we had endured prior to departure that late November day in Indianapolis. Our heavy, black flight suits were soon drenched with sweat in the humid, 85-degree, tropical climate.

A local ground ambulance crew was there to meet us and drove our medical personnel to the hospital to assess Carlos' condition in preparation for his transfer. When we arrived in his room, we were pleasantly surprised to discover that although his body had been severely ravaged by disease, his attitude remained positive. Carlos' son was dutifully stationed right next to his father. He provided heartfelt words of encouragement to his father as we methodically evaluated Carlos and then moved him to our air ambulance cot system.

I watched as Carlos exchanged emotional good-byes with the hospital medical staff who had so diligently cared for him during his long stay there. Several hospital workers, seeing the prominent cross on our flight suits, inquired, "What's Grace on Wings?"

"We're an all-volunteer organization, and our mission is to glorify God by showing the love of Christ through aviation," Tami proudly exclaimed.

One nurse who heard Tami's explanation said, "That's a great mission! We need more people volunteering like you."

After saying our good-byes and transporting Carlos and his son to our aircraft, which we'd named "Nellie," the crew gathered around the cot on which Carlos had been placed. Hal led us in prayer for Carlos and his family. Tears of joy filled the eyes of both Carlos and his son as they experienced the outpouring of love on them from people who just hours before had been complete strangers.

Carlos was then carefully loaded in Nellie's patient transport area and secured for the flight. Carlos' son was seated aboard the plane as well. He was positioned close enough to touch his father's shoulder and speak with him from time to time.

Shortly after takeoff, Carlos said, "I want to thank all of you at Grace on Wings for saving my life."

Not knowing the full story of his illness and all of the trials he had been through, I said simply, "We're glad to be able to help you, Carlos."

With mounting emotion, he said, "Doctor, there's something I need to share with you."

I leaned in to hear his story, knowing his would be the first of many. Each one would be different.

"The doctors at the hospital I just left said nothing more could be done for me. They decided to send me home to be cared for in a hospice program. But when the ambulance attendants put my stretcher on the hydraulic lift to get me into the ambulance, the ramp failed to rise.

"Each time they took me off the lift, it worked normally. But whenever I was put back on the lift, it did not work. The attendants tried three or four times without success. Then someone from the hospital came out to speak to the ambulance attendants. They were told I should remain at the hospital because the situation had changed."

"What do you mean the situation had changed?" I asked.

"My insurance company previously had denied my request for medical care in Indianapolis. Suddenly they decided they would cover those expenses. A new plan would need to be made to get me to Indianapolis. When I heard that news, my faith grew stronger. I knew God was in charge. Instead of going home to die, I was being given a chance to live because God had intervened on my behalf."

"God was at work in Indianapolis too," I said. "He led your brother to Grace on Wings at the same time your insurance company approved your out-of-network care."

Carlos nodded his agreement. "Every day at 10 a.m. I would go to the chapel in the hospital and ask for guidance from God. The morning my insurance company said they would help me, I still had no way to get to Indianapolis. My sister said, 'Carlos, you go to the chapel every day, so let's go there now and pray for God to help you get to Indianapolis.'

"We went to the chapel and prayed, and within thirty minutes I received word that Grace on Wings would take me to get the surgery I needed at St. Vincent Hospital in Indianapolis. I know God made all these things happen. My prayers were answered. No one can make me believe any different."

"God works in powerful and mysterious ways," I said, moved deeply by what he had shared. "I don't think there is any doubt he has plans for your life we cannot yet imagine."

A Chance To Witness

On the northbound flight, we encountered a stiff headwind that burned a lot of fuel and necessitated a refueling stop at an airport just outside of Birmingham, Alabama. As we landed, I saw one of the ground crew at the local airport stare at the red cross on Nellie's tail.

"What does the cross on the plane's tail stand for?" he asked Hal.

Hal's eyes lit up, and a smile broke out on his face. "Brother, that red cross represents the cross that Jesus Christ died on as a sacrifice for the sins of people like you and me."

I listened as Hal shared with the young man how God had blessed him with the vision to serve others through Grace on Wings.

It was a scene I have witnessed countless times since then. Hal boldly proclaims the gospel of Jesus Christ whenever he is given an opportunity such as this one to do so. He is quick to point directly to the cross and tell what Jesus has done for us, not accepting any glory for himself or Grace on Wings. Hal knows, as I do, what wretched creatures we all are before we accept the free gift of salvation through Jesus Christ.

After a full day of travel, Tami and I delivered Carlos to the ICU at St. Vincent Hospital in Indianapolis late that evening. His brother and the surgeon were there to greet him and outline a plan for surgery the following day. The surgeon assured Carlos he would survive but told him he probably would never walk again.

Before leaving Carlos, Tami prayed for God to heal him completely. She promised to visit him after his surgery.

The Rest Of The Story

In the spring of 2013, I contacted Carlos' brother to find out how Carlos was doing. Assuming Carlos must have returned to Florida after his surgery, I was very pleasantly surprised to learn he was living on his own in an apartment in a suburb on the northwest side of Indianapolis. I phoned Carlos, and he agreed to meet with me and tell me the rest of his story.

On May 9, 2013, I went to his small, ground floor apartment in Zionsville, Indiana. Knocking on the door, I heard Carlos yell from inside, "It's open. Come on in, Doctor."

Entering the apartment, I saw Carlos on his feet, slowly shuffling toward me with the assistance of a walker. He smiled profusely and said, "Thank God for Grace on Wings. You guys saved my life!"

"God saved your life," I replied. "He just happened to use us in the process."

We shook hands and embraced before being seated across from each other in the living room of his apartment.

"Carlos, I'm writing a book about the ministry of Grace on Wings. You were our very first patient. I'd like to share your story with others to give them hope in those times when bad things happen in their lives. But I only know half of your story. Please tell me what's happened in your life since we brought you to Indianapolis in 2007."

Carlos beamed his approval.

"First of all, bless you guys for what you did for me," he said. "Also, I need to tell you something you probably won't believe."

He paused and took a deep breath before continuing.

"At one point, while I was under anesthesia during my surgery at St. Vincent Hospital, I saw a man walking ahead of me with a little child. The two of them were holding hands, and they were very happy. I followed them and kept on following them. Everything I was leaving behind was dark, and everything ahead of me was light.

"This man and the little child kept looking at each other and smiling as they walked. At the end of the road, the man turned to the little boy and smiled again. When he did, I suddenly realized the little boy was me when I was a child. I remember the man saying to the child, 'Not yet. Just go and be happy.'

"When I woke up after surgery, my family was around me and they were all crying. 'Why are you crying?' I asked.

"'You were dead!' they said.

"'I'm not dead now. Jesus came to me and said it was not my time to go with him yet,' I told them.

"Most people don't believe me when I tell this story," Carlos said to me. "They say I was hallucinating from the drugs. But I believe it was God telling me something, that I still have a purpose in this life."

"I've heard similar stories from others who've had a near-death experience," I said. "Each one gives me great comfort to know Jesus is waiting in heaven for all of us who have claimed him as our Lord and Savior."

Carlos then went on to tell me what had transpired in the years since then.

"I was in and out of the hospital for several years because my surgical wounds did not heal well. I got treatment at the Rehabilitation Hospital of Indiana and eventually was able to walk again using a walker. My legs were still weak, but I was tired of living in a nursing home or an assisted living facility, so I told my family I wanted to live in my own apartment. They did not think I could do it. But, by God's grace, I have been living here alone now for two years."

"Can you drive a car?" I asked.

"Yes. I can drive using my legs despite everything that has happened to me. I don't go out much because I don't have any friends, just a brother nearby. I stay home most of the time. But I am mostly happy with my life. I have my Bible, and I pray a lot."

"You know, Carlos, we have a Bible study at our Grace on Wings office every Wednesday at noon. Maybe you can join us. I can stop by anytime and pick you up," I said.

"I think I would like that. I need to develop more relationships with other believers and find out what God wants me to do with the rest of my life," he said.

"Your story needs to be told," I said. "Lots of people can gain hope from hearing how God has worked in your life. Your faith is a real inspiration to me, my friend. I hope you will continue to inspire others who are facing difficult situations in life."

After some quiet introspection, Carlos said, "Maybe that is why Jesus told me it was not time to go with him yet."

As I was driving home after my time with Carlos that day, this Scripture came to mind: "'For I know the plans I have for you,' declares the LORD, 'plans to prosper you and not to harm you, plans to give you hope and a future'" (Jeremiah 29:11). I knew God's words to Jeremiah applied not only to Jeremiah and Carlos but also to every one of his children, including Hal, Tami, and me. We had not had a near-death experience like Carlos, but we had indeed been spiritually dead for many years before Jesus gave us new life and a purpose for living. Our stories needed to be told as well.

2

A Prodigal Son Returns
("The Wandering Jew")

W hen Tami and I returned to the Grace on Wings office after transporting Carlos to the hospital following our first mission, Hal was assisting the ground crew in putting the plane into the hangar for the night. When he finished, we again prayed for Carlos and thanked God for the successful launch of our new ministry. I could see how weary Hal was from the physical demands of the long day of flying. The emotional burdens of the day, however, were weighing on him even more.

I knew Hal harbored many concerns about what problems might derail our new organization. As we discussed the first mission and reflected on how we saw God provide for our needs, I could see his anxiety begin to melt away. He had shared the story of his life with me some time back, so I sensed he was still trying to come to grips with a profound question buried deep within his soul. Overcome with emotion, he turned to me and asked, "How could God have chosen to bless me, a prodigal son?"

Growing Up In Brooklyn

Hal Blank was born in the Borough Park region of southwest Brooklyn in the steamy summer of 1959. At that time, the tracks for the L-train divided the crowded neighborhood into discrete ethnic enclaves—Orthodox Jews on one side and Irish and Italians on the other. This urban setting, dominated by a landscape of endless brick and concrete buildings and thoroughfares largely devoid of trees, provided a backdrop to Hal's childhood that was as colorless as an old black-and-white photo of that era.

According to Jewish custom, Hal was named after his paternal grandfather, who had died many years before Hal's birth. Hal's father, a Hasidic Jew, worked as a postmaster for the U.S. Postal service at the JFK airport in Queens. Hal's mother converted from Catholicism to Judaism as a prerequisite to her marriage.

Hal was brought up according to the strict tenets of the Hasidic Jewish religion, which advocated a unique style of dress and physical appearance. A yamaka covered his shaved head, and the traditional long side curls flowed downward over each side of his face. As a consequence of his appearance, he was harassed often by other youths from the non-Jewish communities.

He had been taught that Jews were God's chosen people, and only Jews worshipped in the proper way. He accepted this truth without question. He would walk past the St. Patrick's cathedral near his home, feel the cold air emanating from the cavernous building whenever its doors were open, and not allow himself to look at the church or the people in attendance because he believed Christians were evil and were bound for hell. To avoid being corrupted by the influence of that church, Hal would literally hold his breath for a whole city block as he raced by!

Shortly after the birth of Hal's younger sister in 1966, Hal's parents began to experience marital problems, which subsequently led to a separation and then a divorce in 1968. Hal's mother kept custody of his baby sister but sent Hal to live with his father. Hal's rebelliousness began to surface about this time, and it resulted in significant problems at home and at school. He was constantly in trouble for fighting and for poor performance in his studies.

Outside of school, Hal attempted to cope with his troubled childhood by engaging in reckless behaviors. At the tender age of eight, for example, he decided to take his young girlfriend for an unauthorized and totally illegal joyride in his father's car. After successfully navigating the congested streets of Brooklyn for more than an hour, the seemingly driverless vehicle caught the attention of a passing police patrol car. The incredulous officer riding in the passenger seat of the squad car immediately ordered his partner to stop their vehicle, back up, and investigate the curious sight of a small head barely visible through the steering wheel of Hal's father's car.

Recognizing the impending crisis, Hal gunned the accelerator and sped down the narrow city streets at over 40 mph with the police in hot pursuit. Miraculously Hal avoided a collision, brought the car to a screeching stop, hopped out, and fled the scene as fast as his young legs would carry him. As he did so, he turned and yelled to his frantic girlfriend, "Run!"

Hal managed to evade the police. He hid in various locations around the neighborhood for eight days before returning home to face the wrath of his father and the disdain of the Jewish community.

Further difficulties arose throughout Hal's childhood, culminating in his parents' decision to send him to a private Jewish school in upstate New York in the hope of curbing his mischievous behavior. The private school was very expensive and placed a great financial burden on Hal's father. Fortunately the Jewish community helped defray some of the expense by contributing to Hal's education and support. Hal attended the distant school throughout the week, came home to Brooklyn by train each Friday afternoon, and then returned to school every Sunday evening.

By the time high school graduation rolled around in 1977, Hal knew that he could not afford to attend college. He also knew he could not expect his father to shoulder any further financial burdens on his behalf. He had to make a decision about his future.

As a child, Hal developed a love of aviation as a result of accompanying his father to the JFK airport where his father worked sorting mail for the postal service. He recalled fondly the scene of his father sitting in the living room at home each evening, memorizing postal zip codes on flash cards so he could sort the mail rapidly into the appropriate categories at work. His best memories, however, were of the planes he would watch from the windows of the airport post office.

Hal was fascinated by the multitude of aircraft embarking for exotic locations and returning from distant lands loaded with people from all over the globe. So it seemed logical for him to enlist in the military. There he could pursue training to fly.

In Flight To A New Life

Soon after he finished school, Hal enlisted in the U.S. Army and began to fly helicopters and fixed-wing aircraft at Ft. Rucker, Alabama. By this time, he was essentially living a reformist Jewish lifestyle with no adherence to the religious doctrine of his youth. The required loss of his long hair and beard and the absence of kosher food presented no obstacles to him.

In the military, for the first time, Hal developed friendships with individuals from all walks of life and interacted with many people from a variety of different religious backgrounds. One of Hal's closest friends was a Christian. He would inquire frequently about Hal's Jewish faith and shared with Hal about his relationship with Jesus.

Hal regarded Jesus as a prophet but did not share his friend's belief that Jesus was the Messiah or that Jesus had performed miracles. However, as their friendship progressed over the ensuing years, they had many deep discussions about the Old Testament prophecies regarding the promised Messiah. Through Scripture study, such as Isaiah 53, Hal became curious to know if perhaps his religion might not have told him the whole story of God's plan for creation. He felt prompted in his heart to read the Bible and explore the Scriptures himself to find the truth.

While stationed in Maryland in 1982, Hal experienced his conversion from Judaism to Christianity. He described it as a moment of faith that at first left him initially feeling upset at being left out for so long and then profoundly joyful at being given a pathway to eternal salvation through Jesus Christ. Following his baptism, a new fear gripped him. He realized he could not tell his family about his new faith, as it would result in his being ostracized from those he loved most.

33

Although Hal had observed only the high holidays in the Jewish religion for several years, he still returned home to Brooklyn every September and visited the gravesites of deceased family members with his father. One year after his conversion to Christianity, as Hal and his father stopped for a bagel and coffee at a local neighborhood delicatessen, Hal very subtly bowed his head and silently gave thanks before beginning to eat.

"Is something wrong? Do you feel okay?" Hal's father asked.

Suddenly fearful of disappointing his father by admitting he had become a Christian, Hal said, "What are you talking about? Nothing's wrong. I feel fine."

That weekend Hal continued to deny Christ to avoid a confrontation with his father and the condemnation he feared an admittance of his new faith would bring. Unconvinced and after Hal's third denial, his father exclaimed, "You converted!"

"Yes, Dad, I did," Hal reluctantly admitted.

He expected his father to rip his clothes and declare he no longer had a son. Instead his father simply asked, "What happened?"

Hal told him about his study of both the Old and New Testaments and how he had come to believe Jesus is the Messiah and he had performed all of the miracles recorded in the Bible.

"How are you so sure?" his father questioned.

Recalling Hebrews 11:1, which says, "Now faith is being sure of what we hope for and certain of what we do not see," Hal responded, "By faith, Dad. By faith."

Over the ensuing decades, instead of father and son being driven apart, their relationship gradually deepened as Hal's father recognized the positive influence Hal's new faith had on his life. But such a transformation would take time.

Life as a Christian presented no fewer challenges to Hal than his previous existence had. In an effort to fill a void in his life, Hal married in 1982. He and his wife subsequently had two children, but Hal remained dissatisfied with his life. It seemed that nothing could fill the emptiness inside him.

New Challenges

After several years of flying in the military, Hal sought medical training, first to become an Army medic and then later an orthopedic physician assistant. Little did he know that he would soon be called upon to use his life-saving medical skills in a combat setting.

On October 25, 1983, Hal was one of nearly eight thousand U.S. soldiers to participate in the invasion of the Caribbean island of Grenada. This conflict had been triggered by a bloody military coup and the perceived Soviet-Cuban militarization of the island. Hal's unit parachuted into Grenada under the cover of darkness to secure the main airfield and immediately encountered heavy resistance from Cuban regulars. During the ensuing firefight, an enemy combatant stabbed Hal in the right forearm as he was attending to the injured soldiers in his unit. He responded by emptying his .45-caliber sidearm into his attacker and then resuming his primary duty of stabilizing and evacuating his fallen comrades.

In 1987 Hal was honorably discharged from the Army and was hired as a pilot for Eastern Airlines, flying a shuttle out of the Baltimore/ Washington D.C. region. This position lasted for approximately one year before Eastern Airlines filed for Chapter 11 bankruptcy on March 9, 1989, and went out of business soon thereafter.

Fortunately Hal was able to obtain another job as a pilot, this one flying freight for Chesapeake Air in an MU-2 aircraft out of Baltimore from 1989–1991. During this time, his marital problems came to a head and resulted in Hal and his wife getting a divorce. In his desire to leave behind all of the problems he had faced, Hal took a new job as an orthopedic physician assistant in Mooresville, Indiana, in 1992.

During this time of family upheaval, Hal became very disgruntled and disillusioned with his life and his Christian faith. As a result, he stepped away from his faith and reverted to practicing Judaism by celebrating the high holidays at a local synagogue as he had done in the past. He remained estranged from his ex-wife and his children and resorted to immersing himself in worldly pursuits as he had before he became a Christian.

In the year 2000, Hal began working for the Methodist Hospital system. At that time he came back to the Lord. He began attending services at a church on the north side of Indianapolis, where he immediately felt at home and felt spiritually fed for the first time in many years. It would be another two years before Hal would have his life altered in a major way once again.

Hal And Tami Meet

In 2002, Hal went to Dallas, Texas, to attend an orthopedic conference as part of his continuing medical education. While there, he met a fellow orthopedic physician assistant, Tami, who was also from Indianapolis. Hal and Tami soon discovered they shared many things in common, including a love of the Lord. As they shared their life stories with each other, Hal began to appreciate that he had met someone who had had as difficult a childhood as his.

Over dinner one evening, Tami related to Hal that she had always felt like the forgotten middle child from her mother's first marriage. Her real father had never been a part of her life. Her stepfather did not know how to love her or nurture her. Her mother suffered from severe mental health problems and so was not capable of providing the love and support Tami so desperately needed as a young child. Additionally, the family moved four times during her childhood. It seemed to Tami she constantly had to attend a different school system and struggle to make new friendships wherever she went.

Tami's family did not attend the same church for any length of time before jumping to the next one. Consequently, as a young child, Tami never felt like she understood who God was or experienced his love. Then, when she was set to enroll in the fourth grade, Tami's parents learned that her school was going to start integration by bussing black students to her school. Her parents quickly put Tami in a local Lutheran school to avoid the situation.

Tami told Hal her fourth grade year at the Lutheran school was the best year of her life.

"Really. How so?" Hal said.

"Because I finally met my true Father, God," she replied.

She went on to tell Hal how she vividly remembered the day a missionary came to her school as a guest speaker and told how God was using him to help people in foreign lands. She was so impacted by the missionary she could recall exactly where she was sitting in the classroom that day.

"At that moment," she said, "I knew I wanted to be in the mission field someday."

Although she was later uprooted and moved to another school once again, the seeds had been planted deep in her heart to love God and serve him somehow in the mission field.

As she grew older, Tami tried to win her mother's love and affection by overachieving in her schoolwork and in gymnastics. Her mother, however, was never able to attend any of Tami's gymnastic events because it made her too nervous. Frequently Tami's mom would have to be hospitalized for psychiatric treatment.

In the absence of parental love, Tami searched for acceptance, love, and intimacy from her friends. By the time she was in high school, her faith in God was drastically diminished due to lack of exposure to the Bible and other believers. Instead, peer pressure and worldly pleasures ruled her life.

While in college, Tami found herself facing a major crisis. She became pregnant while she was still unmarried. In desperation, she turned to God for help, and he welcomed her back into his presence. She then was able to help her boyfriend restore his relationship with Jesus as well.

Tami and her boyfriend were subsequently married and had two children together, a girl named Taylor and a boy named Christian. Even as she struggled to raise two young children, Tami went back to school and earned her degree as a physician assistant from Butler University. Unfortunately, marital problems resulted in not one, but eventually two failed marriages.

After graduating from Butler University, Tami worked with a local orthopedic surgeon who also had a heart for foreign missions. At a time when she had just divorced her second husband, Tami felt called to go to El Salvador with a medical team led by her physician employer.

"That's when God reminded me of my call to the mission field," Tami said.

"So what happened next?" Hal asked.

"When I looked into the faces of the natives we went to serve in the mountain villages of Central America," she said, "God showed me his Holy Spirit and renewed my call. But at the same time, I knew I still had two small children to raise and lots of school loans waiting for me at home. So I went home and went back to work, but that missionary spirit remained buried deep within me."

Hal and Tami's First Flight

After the conference in Dallas, Hal and Tami returned to their separate lives in Indianapolis. They continued seeing each other regularly. Hal had shared with Tami that he had been a pilot before moving to Indiana, and she told him that she would like to go for a ride in a plane with him sometime. Although Hal had essentially given up flying when he had lost his plane during his divorce ten years earlier, he decided to surprise Tami by renting a plane to take her flying. It was their first real date.

"Did you pick up flying again to woo the new girl in your life?" Tami asked on the day of the flight.

"Absolutely!" he admitted.

Tami was new to flying and quickly became fascinated with all aspects of aviation as she and Hal continued to date. She was amazed at how comfortable Hal was in flying a number of different aircraft and how knowledgeable he was with anything involving aviation. During their three years of courtship, many of their dates were spent flying.

Hal and Tami were married in 2005. Soon thereafter, Tami began working as a physician assistant in the Emergency Room at Union Hospital in Terre Haute, Indiana. She was anxious to use all of her training and skills by seeing a variety of patients in the ER, not just orthopedic patients as she had done for a number of years.

A Call To Missions

It was not long before my path crossed with Tami. At the time I was working in the ER at Union Hospital as well. Our first meeting was an important one that would shape the future for both of us, and Hal as well.

As she was getting to know the ER staff, Tami learned I had been very involved in Christian mission trips for many years. She read an online blog outlining some of the missionary trips I had led to Peru. As she read, she could hear God's voice calling her to missions once again, this time telling her to go on my next trip to Peru. She recognized she wanted to be involved in missions not only to render medical care but also to share the gospel with others.

Tami shared her missionary desires with Hal, and he was intrigued with the idea of foreign mission work. Tami felt his initial motivation was simply to go along to protect his new wife of less than one year. Nevertheless, they began dreaming about a way to combine Hal's aviation skills and their medical skills into some sort of mission endeavor. Admittedly, their motivation at that point was more focused on obtaining an aircraft they could use for recreational purposes than seeking God's direction in their lives.

In preparation for the mission trip to Peru, Tami read the book, *Dream Giver*, by Bruce Wilkerson. The book spoke to her so intimately it was like she could hear the Holy Spirit speaking directly to her. Wilkerson said in the book that God gives each of us a "big dream" to fulfill in life. Further, it said we would not feel complete without doing what God has prepared and called us to do. Tami knew her big dream would somehow involve aviation and missions, but at that time, only God knew the plans he had in store for her and Hal.

3

Lean Not On Your Own Wisdom
("Me, A Doctor? Didn't See That Coming!")

Tami Blank and I began working together in the emergency room at Union Hospital in Terre Haute, Indiana, during the summer of 2005. She was a petite young woman, measuring all of four feet ten inches tall although she will always say she is five feet tall if you ask her.

When we first met, she radiated a friendly smile. "Dr. Jim, I hear you lead mission trips to South America every year. I would like to join you when you go next time."

She must have sensed some skepticism from my demeanor because she quickly added, "I know you probably have a lot of people say they are interested in going on a mission trip with you and then back out. But my husband and I are serious about becoming more involved in mission work. And we would like to take our 13-year-old daughter, Taylor, with us as well—if you allow teenagers to go."

Indeed I had experienced many individuals express an initial excitement about going on a foreign mission trip only to lose that enthusiasm and never follow through. I had been leading mission teams from my church to Peru each year since 1999. The allure of a foreign mission trip, I learned, was often lost when the financial costs and the demands of the trip became real.

"The next trip to Peru will be in June of 2006, and you and your husband and daughter are certainly welcome to be a part of the team. I'll let you know more details about the definite trip dates and itinerary in early spring when we have a callout meeting."

After that initial encounter, I worked with Tami frequently and was impressed by the compassion she exhibited to patients. From time to time, she would remind me of her commitment to go to Peru, and I would reassure her there was room for anyone being called by God to be a part of his work there. Reflecting on my own past, I knew I was living proof.

My Early Years

My upbringing was not atypical for a child born in the Midwest in 1953. I was raised in Forrest, Illinois, a small, rural town surrounded by endless cornfields interspersed with acres upon acres of soybeans.

We didn't live on a farm, so I was free to spend most of my time in the company of a few close friends, engaged in the usual pursuits of boyhood. We maintained a state of perpetual motion while playing whichever sport was in season, racing through town on bikes or on foot, and continually pursuing the affections of young ladies with whom we were smitten.

My parents believed very strongly I needed to attend Sunday school and church each week at the only Methodist church in town. They, however, rarely attended any church service and did not lead lives consistent with the teachings of Christianity. They were good people, normal people in the eyes of the world, but definitely not Christians. Consequently, religion was not a high priority in my life at that time.

My father had worked at a local tile factory since returning home from military service after World War II, and my mother worked as a telephone switchboard operator. We were not poor by any means, but I was encouraged to work hard for whatever I wanted. Money was tight, and the value of hard work was highly esteemed.

By the time I was ten years old, I was delivering newspapers and mowing lawns to earn spending money. During the summers I would work on local farms, "walking beans" or baling hay for a dollar an hour. The easier of the two was the bean job, which involved walking the rows of beans and pulling out weeds—pigweed, smartweed, and butterprint—by hand.

During my last two years of high school, I was up at 5 a.m. each morning, Monday through Saturday, to work as a milkman. I delivered dairy products door to door throughout the town as well as to local schools and restaurants. Some weeknights and weekends were spent pumping gas at Toby's Sinclair gas station on the north end of town. But even with the jobs and the money I saved, a college education was beyond my reach.

The stories told around the dinner table that I most remember related to my father's experiences when he served in the U.S. Army. In fact, most of the men I knew in my youth had served in the military and were proud of their service for our country.

One cousin, who was like an older brother to me, had served as a paratrooper with the 173rd Airborne in Vietnam. Two other cousins had been stationed in Thailand during their four-year stints in the Air Force. So it seemed natural for me to join the military after graduating from high school in 1971. The GI Bill would be used to pay for my college education when I completed my time in the service.

Since I was still only seventeen in May of 1971, the Air Force required my parents' approval before I could be inducted into the military. My parents reluctantly agreed it was a reasonable and honorable way for me to move forward with my life. Three days after graduation from high school, I left home for basic training at Lackland Air Force Base in San Antonio, Texas.

B-52 Tail Gunner

During basic training, the Air Force determines what career field each airman will be assigned to. Because I had scored very high on the electronics section of my placement tests, I qualified for several flying jobs. When I inquired about the flying opportunities, the sergeant said one such job was Defensive Fire Control Systems Operator.

"What's that?" I asked.

"You sit in front of a panel of circuit breakers and put out fires on the plane," he replied.

Now I wasn't very knowledgeable about planes, but I wanted to fly, and I thought I could pull circuit breakers. So I said, "I want to be a Defensive Fire Control Systems Operator." Little did I know at the time it was a fancy name for a tail gunner on a B-52 bomber!

My ignorance was actually a huge blessing in my life. As a tail gunner, I was the only enlisted man on a crew with five officers. Each pilot, copilot, radar navigator (bombardier), navigator, and electronic warfare officer was a college graduate with lots of maturity and wisdom to pass along to a young man seeking his place in the world. Every one of them gave me the same advice. "Jim, when you get out of the service, use the GI Bill to go to college."

I planned to heed that advice, but at the time I had no clue as to what to do with my life or what career to pursue.

After completing my flight training in California in March of 1972, I was stationed at Wright-Patterson Air Force Base in Dayton, Ohio. My crew flew extensive training missions, and we were also required to be on nuclear alert. The rigorous training I received under stressful circumstances served me well by developing in me a character of toughness and decisiveness. These attributes would be invaluable in dealing with medical emergencies in the ER and with Grace on Wings flights many years later.

In the spring of 1972, the Vietnam War was still dragging on with no acceptable end in sight. B-52s had been used to bomb military targets throughout Southeast Asia beginning in 1965. However, B-52s had never been called upon to fly over the heavily defended regions of North Vietnam, where deadly, Soviet-made SA-2 surface-to-air missiles were concentrated. That precedent was about to change.

President Nixon was attempting to extract the U.S from the war with honor and win the release of all our POWs. Some five hundred American soldiers were being held captive in POW camps located mainly in Hanoi, North Vietnam. After the repeated failure of peace negotiations, Nixon stepped up military attacks throughout South Vietnam and ordered the redeployment of hundreds of B-52s.

Bombers, crews, and support personnel were sent to Anderson AFB on the island of Guam and to the Royal Thai Naval Base at

Utapao, Thailand. The stage was being set for the final act in the U.S. involvement in the decade long war in Vietnam. For me, the stage was being set for a future that would involve extensive air travel, not for the military, but for the Lord.

At the time, my main fear was the war would be over before I had a chance to take part in it. After all, I had been training for this opportunity since joining the Air Force. Having heard the war stories from the veterans who had "been there," I wanted to experience the war myself.

In my youthful exuberance, I volunteered to change crews to fill an opening on another Wright-Patterson crew scheduled to deploy to Southeast Asia in October of 1972. The Squadron Commander, however, chose to keep my crew intact and filled that open gunner position with one of my roommates, Al Moore. I was a bit resentful that Al, who had finished training after me, would get to Guam and Thailand before I would.

Guam

My crew finally left California on December 16, 1972. We flew a B-52D to Anderson AFB on the island of Guam, a U.S. territory in the Mariana Islands located three thousand miles from the coast of Vietnam. The island, thirty miles long and eleven miles wide, was just a tiny speck of land in the middle of the Pacific Ocean. Crossing the International Dateline, we landed on Guam at approximately 0215 hours local time on the morning of December 18, joining more than one thousand other B-52 crewmembers already in place for what was ahead.

When the door to my gunner's compartment was opened, the stifling heat and humidity immediately overwhelmed me. Jumping down onto the tarmac, I noticed the entire flight line was a beehive of activity. Over a hundred and fifty B-52s were parked in revetments all up and down the taxiways with their huge vertical stabilizers jutting into the sky like the fins of so many sharks silhouetted against the horizon. At the time, I did not realize I was witnessing the massive preparation for the biggest aerial assault since the bombing of Germany during World War II.

Later that day, as the sinking sun painted its idyllic colors on the western horizon, the calm atmosphere was broken by the unmistakable roar of eight powerful jet engines propelling a B-52 down the two-mile long runway at Anderson AFB. I knew the sound of the B-52 engines, so I was not surprised by the initial disturbance. But the perpetual launching of one bomber after another continued for over two hours without interruption. Even a rookie like me knew that was not standard operating procedure!

Early the next day, December 19, 1972, we began to see the B-52s returning to Guam after a nearly fourteen-hour bombing mission. The parade of planes coming home continued for several hours and then suddenly ceased.

"The Eleven Day War"

My crew was summoned to a meeting at the base that afternoon to receive our initial orientation. The general giving the briefing explained what had transpired the previous day. The aircrews I'd watched taking off had been given their target for the night's bombing mission. It was Hanoi, North Vietnam!

The United States had never flown bombing missions over such a heavily defended target with the B-52. Nixon, however, hoped to force the enemy into submission and coerce them into agreeing to a peace treaty involving the release of all of our POWs from captivity. And until December 18, 1972, no B-52s had ever been lost to hostile fire during the entirety of the Vietnam War.

The period from December 18–30, 1972, has been called the "Eleven Day War," although the official name was "Linebacker II." During those tragic eleven days, fifteen B52s were lost to enemy fire. A total of thirty-three crewmen were killed, and another thirty-four airmen became POWs. Something died inside of me then as well. The innocence of youth and the feeling of invincibility vanished as I faced my own mortality for the first time.

My crew was fortunate. The two missions we flew during that perilous time were easy compared to the dangers experienced by some of my friends who never returned. Nevertheless, the reality of death awakened in me a desire to draw near to the God I had ignored for much of my life. That desire would wane again as my circumstances improved.

Although the price of victory was costly and painful, the bombings did achieve the desired result. The North Vietnamese signed the Paris Peace Treaty on January 28, 1973, officially ending the role of the United States in the Vietnam War. Most importantly, within two months after the signing of the peace treaty, all our POWs were liberated.

Shortly after the bombing of North Vietnam ceased, I ran into my roommate from Wright-Patterson, Al Moore. Al's crew had been sent to Guam from Thailand before returning to the U.S. A lot had happened since we had last seen each other several months before. We found a quiet spot on the beach, cracked open a bottle of bourbon, and spent the whole night talking about the war and what it might mean to our future.

Al told me he and his crew had been stationed at Utapao, Thailand, when the raids over Hanoi began. They flew a total of seven of the eleven nights. I knew Al had shot down a Mig-21 over Hanoi on Christmas Eve, so I pressed him for details of the event. He reluctantly gave me a brief recap of his combat encounter with the enemy fighter. Then he said, "I was just doing my job. You know, there was a guy in that Mig. I'm sure he would have wanted to fly home too. But it was a case of him or my crew."

Soon thereafter, my crew and I were sent to Thailand for the remainder of our overseas tour. Al and I remained good friends and got together from time to time through the years. But I never again heard him talk about his combat experience.

In the spring of 2009, Al's ex-wife called me. She told me Al was dying of lung cancer and was on hospice care. She wanted to let me know in the hope some of Al's old war buddies might be able to contact him to say their good-byes.

Al was not a Christian when we last met, and I did not know if his ex-wife was a believer. But I felt compelled to ask her if Al had made his peace with God. I was much relieved to hear he had given his life to Christ and was prepared to meet his Lord and Savior. My subsequent phone conversations with Al were brief because of his weakened state, but we did pray together before he died.

I sometimes wonder what my life would have been like had I filled that open gunner position instead of Al. Would I have flown those seven missions over Hanoi and shot down a Mig-21 as Al had done? Or would I have been shot down and had my life terminated many years before the time when I gave my life to Jesus? No matter how many times I wrestle with those questions, I find no answers.

A New Direction

The simplicity of life and the friendliness of the people in Thailand had made a lasting impression on me. The impact was so great I volunteered to return for three more tours of duty after my first six months there. During my last few months in Thailand, and with less than a year remaining before my discharge from the service, God gave me a calling for the rest of my life. It was an unexpected change of direction, one I didn't acknowledge then as coming from him.

A Thai friend of mine was severely injured in an automobile accident. When I went to visit him in the local hospital, I was appalled at the archaic hospital facilities and primitive medical care he was receiving. Although it was probably standard treatment in that area, I felt called to become a physician and return to Thailand to help improve medical care to the indigent people.

I can't ever remember entertaining the thought of becoming a doctor before that time. In retrospect, having walked with the Lord for a quarter of a century since 1988, I can see how he was at work in my life long before I knew him as my Savior.

When I returned to the United States after my final overseas tour, I immediately began exploring medicine as a career. Learning that Southern Illinois University had just recently opened a new medical school, I enrolled as an undergraduate student majoring in Physiology at SIU-Carbondale. I began summer school shortly after my discharge from the military.

I was driven by my personal desire to succeed in getting accepted to medical school and returning to Thailand as expeditiously as possible. I would soon come to realize God had other plans for my life.

Proverbs 3:5–6 says, "Trust in the LORD with all your heart and lean not on your own understanding; in all your ways acknowledge him, and he will make your paths straight." Looking back on those times, I now see how God was at work in my life. He was preparing me for the work he would call me to years later.

4

Stepping Out In Faith
("You Want Me To Go Where?")

My journey to become Medical Director for Grace on Wings was still unfolding before me. God had a great deal to teach me and show me.

One day in the fall of 1975, I received an important phone call from my sister, Karen. She informed me that Becky Sans, a girl I had met four years previously at a high school basketball game, had just moved back to her hometown following the death of her husband in a motorcycle accident in California.

I was surprised to hear the news. Becky and I had made a connection that night. We communicated by mail a few times in the spring of 1971 before I joined the Air Force. We lost touch, and she subsequently married and had a baby.

After Karen's call, I contacted Becky, and soon thereafter we had our first date. We spent the evening sharing everything that had happened in our lives during the past few years. God was unexpectedly bringing us together again four and a half years after we first met.

Becky, now my wife of thirty-five years, still remembers how passionately I shared my dreams of becoming a doctor and returning to Thailand to serve the people there. Nearly forty years had gone by since I left Thailand, and I still not returned. But I'd had the privilege

49

of becoming a physician and serving the needy throughout the world in Ecuador, Peru, Haiti, Zambia, Pakistan, Iraq, and Liberia. I now realize God is more interested in my obedience to his will than my dreams of how I want my life to go.

When I was accepted into medical school in 1978, Becky and I were married. The next ten years were filled with the demands of medical school, residency, developing my private practice, and starting a family. God was not a priority in our lives. Although Becky and I considered ourselves Christians, neither of us yet had experienced a life-changing relationship with Jesus.

On the outside I had everything I thought would make me happy—a good job, a nice house, and a wonderful family with three beautiful children. Yet despite all of my worldly success, I felt hollow inside. I was living a very self-centered and self-destructive lifestyle. The abuse of work, alcohol, and prescription drugs failed to fill the void deep inside me. Instead, my physical and mental health suffered tremendously, causing a burden on my marriage and my work.

Only after much pain and sorrow would I learn my emptiness could only be filled by God. A quote from a nineteenth-century English missionary, Henry Martyn, best characterized my condition in life at that time. "I obtained my highest wishes, but was surprised to find that I had grasped only a shadow."

Born Again

God allowed me to suffer the consequences of my actions until December of 1988, when at last I surrendered my life to him. In that moment when I accepted Jesus as Lord and Savior, I immediately felt a burden lifted from my shoulders. A sense of peace like I had never known before began to grow within me. And a call to mission service was about to be born.

Becky was elated with my newfound faith in the Lord. Although she could not remember a specific moment of salvation, Becky felt secure in her own relationship with God. She had longed for a husband who would share her beliefs and provide spiritual leadership in our home.

As we became more involved with church activities, she prayed my spiritual conversion would lead to a lifetime of walking with the Lord. I confided in her the desire I felt to become engaged in medical missions to people in the poorer countries around the world. At that time, however, the duties of everyday life made it impossible.

In the summer of 1989, Becky and I felt God calling us to the town of Frankfort, Indiana, where I had been offered a job as Emergency Room Medical Director at the Clinton County Hospital. A year later, our family was invited to attend church services at the First Presbyterian Church in Frankfort. This church had welcomed a new pastor, Pat Smith, just six months previous to our initial visit. We were overwhelmed by the friendliness of everyone we met and truly felt God had led us to this congregation to worship and serve him.

Pastor Pat came to our home shortly after we indicated we would like to join the church. He asked me pointedly, "Jim, where do you see yourself serving God within the church?"

I told him about my experiences in Thailand and the call I felt to perform medical work in Third World countries. I assumed there would be many opportunities for medical mission work through the church. He listened patiently and prayed with us.

My knowledge of the Bible was almost nonexistent at the time, since I had not yet begun to study God's Word intentionally. Oh, I had tried to read the Bible in times of distress before I gave my life to Jesus. In the past, when life seemed hopeless and the darkness of depression seemed to surround me, I had sought for relief in God's Word. But without the gift of the Holy Spirit, which God gives each person who professes Jesus as Lord and Savior, the Bible had made little sense to me.

Fortunately for me, Pastor Pat and his wife, Laura, had just begun teaching *Precept Upon Precept* Bible studies by Kay Arthur. He invited us to join in the class. Becky and I were thrilled to have a formal study that introduced us to the Bible and also taught us how to inductively study it on our own.

My first mission experiences were as a member of nonmedical mission teams to Appalachia, the Dominican Republic, and Russia.

I continued to look for opportunities to be involved in medical mission work through the church, but nothing materialized.

As I studied God's Word and came to know him better, however, I realized I was not ready to be sent out into the medical missions field. God didn't want me just to heal people's bodies, but also to heal them spiritually by introducing them to the Great Physician, Jesus.

New Opportunities

In 1998 I felt called to take a new job in an urgent care center in Lafayette, Indiana. Although not understanding the reason I felt compelled to change, I was convinced God wanted me to make this move.

On the first day of my new job a colleague asked me, "Are you a member of the Christian Medical and Dental Society?"

"No. I've never heard of it," I said.

He proceeded to tell me the CMDS performs medical mission work all over the world. He gave me the website address and urged me to look into it.

There was no doubt in my mind. I had just discovered the reason God called me to my new job! God had spoken directly to me through a brother in Christ. He had heard and answered my prayers for a way to serve in medical mission trips overseas. I could hardly wait to get home and check out the CMDS website and see what mission opportunities were available.

That night I examined the website and was immediately drawn to a notice advertising a medical mission trip on a riverboat called "The Chosen Vessel" on the Amazon River in Peru. It read, "Awake to find our ship docked beside a pueblo of the Amazon. Have breakfast together before walking to the pueblo to begin providing medical attention and presenting the Good News of the Gospel of Christ to the village." I was sure God wanted me on that particular exotic adventure!

When I contacted the CMDS office the following day, I was told the Amazon River mission trip was already filled. I was disappointed but asked, "Where do you have the greatest need?"

The CMDS secretary said, "We need doctors to serve in the prisons in Ecuador."

Serving in the prisons in Ecuador didn't sound nearly as appealing to me as floating up and down the Amazon River on a comfortable medical ship! But I knew God had answered my prayers. He had led me to this point where a definite need existed, and I had an opportunity to serve, albeit not in the way or the place I might have chosen.

I John 5:3 says, "This is love for God: to obey his commands." I knew God had been preparing me for that opportunity to serve, and I needed to obey his call.

"Sign me up!" I said.

Ecuador

In the spring of 1998, a group of Christian doctors, nurses, dentists, pharmacists, and others from all across the United States traveled together to Ecuador as a medical mission team under the direction of the CMDS. We were scheduled to provide medical care to inmates in the federal prisons in Guayaquil, Quito, Latacunga, and Rio Bamba. Local translators were provided to assist us in communicating with our patients.

During that two-week trip, we were able to provide needed medical care to many inmates. But more importantly, we were able to pray with them and show them the love of Christ, something many had never experienced before. Although separated by a language barrier, I could sense the inmates' gratitude in response to even the smallest act of kindness. The prison may not have changed as a result of our visit, but I felt the hearts of those we served had been altered forever.

My heart had been changed as well. For the first time I truly realized my role was not to convert everyone to Christianity. That was God's business. Instead, I was to love people unconditionally just as Jesus did. It was a lesson I would apply constantly in the future in dealing with patients in the ER and Grace on Wings. I could not save anyone's life, but I could show everyone the love of Christ.

After I returned home from my first medical mission trip, Becky and I were presented with an opportunity to host a foreign exchange student named Adriana. She was from Manta, Ecuador. Truthfully, I had never thought about Ecuador at any point in my life, and yet within a few months, God had drawn me to Ecuador in multiple ways. We agreed to host Adriana for a year.

At the same time, Becky and I both signed up for a CMDS medical mission trip to serve the Quechua Indians in the remote Andes Mountains in Ecuador. Ironically, soon after Adriana was settled into our home in Frankfort, Indiana, Becky and I visited Adriana's family in Manta, Ecuador, just prior to the start of our mission work with the Quechua. It was a blessing to meet Adriana's family and share our lives with them. Because of the relationship we formed with the family, Adriana's younger brother, Gustavo, would also spend a year in our home as an exchange student the following year.

Becky had been involved in yearly mission trips through our church since 1992, when she helped in the cleanup of Homestead, Florida, after Hurricane Andrew. In subsequent years, she was a part of a mission team to the Yucatan Peninsula region of Mexico, where our church had been helping the people in a small Presbyterian church in the Mayan pueblo of Nohchakan. The trip to serve the Quechua in Ecuador, however, was Becky's first foreign mission experience outside of Mexico.

I have many fond memories of that trip, but one in particular stands out above all the rest. Our group had traveled a very narrow, winding, treacherous mountain road to get to a remote Quechua village where people from all over the countryside were converging to seek medical care from the "gringo" doctors. As we set up small wooden desks for the doctors and plastic chairs for the patients in our makeshift medical "offices" outdoors on the side of the mountain, I looked across the steep valley and saw the clouds actually floating by below us. We were at nearly 12,000 feet elevation, and the thin air was cold and damp.

As I examined patients, I wondered what my wife was doing. One of Becky's concerns on this trip was how she would be able to help, since she had no medical training. But I knew she had the spiritual gift of loving unconditionally, especially children. I was confident God would use her gift according to his will.

After seeing a number of patients, I wandered over to where we had parked the dilapidated bus that brought us to this mountain paradise. There, on the far side of the vehicle, I saw Becky lovingly washing the dirty, calloused, deformed feet of Quechua children and fitting them with new pairs of shoes! A perpetual smile graced her face, and tears of joy and compassion filled her eyes as she loved the children of the village in a way she could not have imagined before that day.

Normally the Quechua children went barefoot despite the rugged terrain and frigid temperature, or they wore the same pair of shoes for years. What a blessing it was for our team to donate shoes to those children. God showed us he uses all those whom he has called. Our job was to make ourselves available to participate in his work and obey him whenever he called. It was a lesson that would serve me well when the time came for me to join Grace on Wings.

Peruvian Jungle Trip

At the beginning of 1999, I was asked to lead the Mission Team at First Presbyterian Church. A $6,000 line item was in the mission budget for beginning a ministry with an "unreached people group." Someone on the team explained that Reverend Dan McNerney, a member of Presbyterian Frontier Fellowship, had given the team a book containing hundreds of unreached people groups around the world. It became our task to discern which unreached people group God wanted us to minister to and how we could use our resources to make Jesus known to them.

After several team meetings and much prayer, we were not feeling led to any particular group. So I called Reverend McNerney and explained our frustration to him.

"Jim, I am leaving for a trip to Peru in the next few days. Let's get together when I return and see if we can find an unreached people group for your church," he said.

When Dan returned to his home in Chicago several weeks later, he phoned me. "You are not going to believe this," he said, "but I think I know which unreached people group God wants you to work with!" He said he had met the pastor of the Presbyterian Church in Moyobamba, a small city in the high jungle region of northern Peru. Pastor Persin was looking to reach the nearby Aguaruna Indians with the gospel, but his church wanted to partner with a U.S. church to assist in this venture.

It didn't take a lot of imagination to see how God was at work to bring our two churches together to accomplish his work. The mission team heard the story Dan had related to me. They felt we should partner with the Presbyterian Church in Moyobamba, Peru, by adopting the Aguaruna Indians as our unreached people group.

I researched the Aguaruna Indians and discovered they were a large group of hunter-gatherers located throughout the Amazon jungle in northern Peru. Previous missionary work had been done among them over the preceding fifty years by Wycliffe linguists and translators. One missionary had lived among them for over twenty-five years and had written a book, *Treasures in Clay Pots*, which detailed her work.

In spite of this earlier work, the Moyobamba congregation assured us there still was no viable church in the Aguaruna communities they were seeking to reach. The church Mission Team decided the only way for us to know for sure if this group was our assignment from the Lord was for someone from our church to go to Moyobamba and establish a personal relationship with our brothers and sisters there. It seemed as though I could hear God saying to me, "Now you may go to the Amazon region of Peru!"

Local fireman and church member Craig Rutledge and I arrived in Moyobamba in August of 1999 after nearly two full days of travel by air and ground. During our fact-finding expedition, we were to visit several Aguaruna communities, meet with the leaders of the Moyobamba church, and discuss with them how our two churches might partner to accomplish their vision.

First, we were taken to the home of a local parishioner who had graciously opened up his home to Craig and me. Later that night, as we sat around a table in the dimly lit dining room, Pastor Persin outlined the itinerary for our trek through the jungle the next day. He said we must leave at dawn and travel upriver into the jungle in a small boat in order to arrive at the distant Aguaruna village of Nueva Vida by nightfall. After spending the night in an Aguaruna hut, we would travel on foot to the remote native community of Kusu the following day.

Pastor Persin emphasized this part of the journey could be very difficult and dangerous, as the jungle path led through expansive marshes. We would need to cross many streams and rivers. He paused for a moment and then said, "There are many boas in the water. So you must not fall in. They usually eat only one, but they do have a taste for gringos!"

He got a good laugh out of that, but all I got was nightmares. I did not get much sleep that night. I continuously saw huge boa constrictors lunging toward me from the marshes whenever I closed my eyes.

The next morning we were met by Pastor Persin and four other Peruvians who would be going into the jungle with us. Victor and Elizabeth Vargas and two of their children, Hans and Leslie, would be cooking our meals and making sure we did not get eaten by a boa.

The journey through the jungle lasted for nearly four days and was very physically demanding. The Aguaruna leaders seemed genuinely enthusiastic about establishing churches in their communities. Craig and I returned home with the assurance that God was indeed calling us to partner with our new friends to grow his church in the remote Amazonian jungle. Little did I know my first mission trip to Peru would bless me in so many ways and prepare me for my work with Grace on Wings.

First Mission Trip To Peru

Becky accompanied me, along with ten others from our church, on the first working trip to Peru in 2000. The following year, our 20-year-old daughter, Angie, and 19-year-old son, Dustin, were part of the mission team to Peru. Then in 2002, Angie spent the summer living with Victor and Elizabeth Vargas as an immersion experience to improve her Spanish language skills. The Vargas family had become dear friends of ours by then.

During that summer, Angie met Hans Vargas for the first time when he came home for a visit during a break from his college studies. They told me it was love at first sight. All who witnessed their relationship, especially their parents, can testify it was God who brought them together.

After a four-year courtship, Hans and Angie were married in 2006, and they brought two beautiful children, Ian and Kira, into the world. I never could have imagined I would gain a godly son-in-law and two wonderful grandchildren as a result of making a mission trip to Peru!

Ephesians 3:20–21 says, "Now to him who is able to do immeasurably more than all we ask or imagine, according to his power that is at work within us, to him be glory in the church and in Christ Jesus throughout all generations, for ever and ever!" To me this verse means God has promised to bless us when we obey him because he loves us. But we must take the first step in faith when we hear his call. Then we can rejoice as he blesses us in ways we could not have imagined when we answered his call to service.

Since that first mission trip to Peru, I have learned that just one call to action is probably not the only one to come in a lifetime. That one mountain or jungle just conquered will look like child's play compared to what God calls us to next.

5

Crisis Of Belief
("Hal Must Be Crazy!")

Hal and Tami Blank had said they felt called to be a part of the mission team to Peru in June of 2006, and their interest lasted beyond the initial excitement and the challenges of cost and time commitment. The three of us got to know each other during the trip-planning sessions in the spring of that year.

When I first met with Hal, he shared he had been a pilot in the military and later in the commercial airline industry before beginning a career as an orthopedic physician assistant. He also shared how he and Tami met and their desire to be involved in mission work by combining their skills in aviation and medicine.

With that background in mind, I asked them if they wanted to meet missionary friends of ours serving as bush pilots for South American Air ministry (SAMAIR) in Pucallpa, Peru. They were indeed anxious to get to know missionary pilots doing what they had been dreaming of for years.

One of the primary projects for our team, I told Hal and Tami, would be to perform medical clinics in Aguaruna Indian communities deep in the Amazonian jungle. The idea of having two physician assistants with me as we tended to patients in the remote villages was very appealing. Hal and Tami were eager to experience the native culture and provide medical care to people who may have never seen a doctor before. I could see the excitement building in them as the departure date drew near.

As it turned out, Hal and Tami and their daughter, Taylor, were the most enthusiastic members of our Peru mission team. At age thirteen, Taylor was the youngest team member I had ever taken to Peru. My hope was that she would be able to develop relationships with the Peruvian youth in a way we had never been able to, and she did.

It was always refreshing for me to see the joy in the faces of the team members as they experienced God's blessings during their mission trip. Tami and Taylor sported smiles from ear to ear throughout the trip as they helped the Peruvian people in any way they could. The medical clinics were a huge success in large part because of the dedication of Hal and Tami. Their expertise in treating all sorts of parasitic infections, skin lesions, and orthopedic problems was invaluable. And they did it all with love.

Sitting next to Hal in the airplane on the return flight home, I listened as he shared how God had spoken to him during his time there. He said he sensed God calling him to become involved in some sort of full-time aviation ministry.

During the trip, Hal and Tami met my missionary friends the bush pilots working with SAMAIR. Hal was enamored with their ministry. He knew he could not fill that role, however, since he did not speak Spanish and had not received the required extensive flight training through Moody Bible Institute flight school.

As Hal and I continued to talk about his experiences in Peru, I could see he had been truly impacted by the trip, but I had no idea God had grabbed hold of him so completely. Nor did I ever imagine what was about to unfold.

Following the trip to Peru, I concentrated on passing my medical board recertification exam, working in the ER, and attending the two weddings for my daughter Angie and her fiancé, Hans—one ceremony in Peru and another in the U.S. I didn't see or talk to Hal again for several months.

Birth Of A Ministry

One day at work several months after the Peru trip, Tami told me she and Hal were establishing a new 501(c)(3) nonprofit organization to provide charity air ambulance services to people in need here in the Midwest. God had opened her eyes, she explained, to the needs of some of her orthopedic patients here in Indiana, needs she thought could be met only by establishing this new mission organization.

I already knew about Hal's dream to be involved in full-time aviation ministry from our conversation on the flight home. And now Tami was sharing she had come back from Peru with a renewed desire to be a missionary and felt the Holy Spirit calling her to this ministry.

After discussing the situation with their pastor, Gary Walker, Tami said she and Hal had become convinced God had answered their prayers and given them the vision for a new ministry. Gary agreed to become a board member for their new organization while also remaining their spiritual advisor, and then the three of them proceeded to prepare the required paperwork needed to incorporate this new organization. But first they had to come up with a name for the new ministry.

Tami then related how the name Grace on Wings was born. As she and Hal had prayed about what to call the new organization, she kept thinking about how God had led them to that moment. She knew the opportunity to use aviation in ministry was a gift from God that they had done nothing to deserve. It was by grace alone. The word *grace* kept echoing in her mind.

One day as she and Hal were driving out of their subdivision in separate vehicles, Tami suddenly stopped her car in the middle of the road. A startled Hal watched as Tami jumped out and ran back to his car.

"What's the matter? Are you okay?" he asked.

"Grace on Wings! We'll call it Grace on Wings! It just came to me!"

"Honey, that's perfect! Praise God! I love it!"

Next Tami began to tinker around on the computer as she tried to come up with a logo. She decided it should contain the ministry name along with a red cross signifying the blood of Christ shed on Calvary for the remission of sins. She then pictured an aircraft writing the words *Grace on Wings* in the sky.

Suddenly there it was! She was certain the Holy Spirit had given her the vision for a logo that would forever be associated with the ministry of Grace on Wings.

I was only half listening when Tami started telling me her story. My thoughts were more focused on the patients I had just seen and those still waiting to be seen. Seeing her excitement, however, I finally realized something major was happening as her tale unfolded. When she finished, I didn't exactly know what to say.

"You're really serious about this?" I asked.

"Yes. Isn't it great?"

A million questions were racing through my head as I tried to catch up with where Hal and Tami had gotten to since the trip to Peru. I hadn't yet connected all the dots. In fact, a part of me said the dots couldn't possibly be connected. The whole idea sounded a bit grandiose.

"Yes. It sounds fantastic," I said. "Let me know how it goes."

Invitation To A God-sized Project

A few days after my conversation with Tami, Hal called me. He said he'd heard what Tami had shared with me and thought we should talk.

"Hal, I didn't really understand what Tami was telling me," I said.

"Which part?" he asked.

"Well, just about all of it, I guess. I know you guys had a great experience in Peru, but are sure you know what you're doing?"

I felt stupid as soon as those words left my mouth. Some faith I had!

"Jim, I've never been more sure of anything in my life. God put this on our hearts, and we need to do it. Tami and I are convinced of that," Hal said.

He explained everything that had happened since the trip to Peru, and then he shared with me his vision for Grace on Wings.

"Hal, this is big. This is huge, man," I said.

"You're telling me, brother. I haven't slept for weeks!"

"I don't know a thing about air ambulances. Are you sure there is a need for what you are proposing?"

"We checked it out and were told there's no charity air ambulance service in the country."

"What's this about starting a nonprofit organization?" I asked. "I thought only churches and big companies did that."

"We don't want this to be about a church. This is about showing Christ's love to everyone. We have to be our own organization."

"What about an airplane?" I asked.

"We'll have to buy one."

"How much will that cost?" I asked.

"We can get an MU-2 for somewhere around $300,000 to $400,000."

By then my palms were sweating profusely. Although I was intrigued by what he was proposing to do, I didn't really understand how he could attempt such a huge project.

"That's a lot of money, Hal. Where are you going to come up with it?"

"I don't know. We'll have to trust God to provide it for us," he said.

I didn't anticipate what he would say next.

"Jim, we are going to need a medical director, and I would like you to pray about filling that position for Grace on Wings."

A flood of emotions swept over me. I was excited and honored to think that Hal and Tami would ask me to become involved in their new organization. At the same time, fear and uncertainty overwhelmed me as I realized that the details and demands of this new role were totally unknown. So I did what most Christians do when stalling for time.

"I'll pray about it!" I said.

A decision this big would require not only a lot of prayer but a serious discussion with my wife. I could hardly wait to get home that evening and share the news.

"Hal must be crazy!" was Becky's response.

Well, maybe she didn't say those exact words, but they are what I distinctly heard when I told her about my conversation with Hal.

To be completely truthful, I must admit a somewhat similar thought had crossed my mind when first Hal told me what God was calling him to do. Not "crazy" in the usual sense of the word perhaps, but more a recognition of how monumental the task of starting a nonprofit air ambulance service would be.

Becky understood without saying so that something major was taking place in our lives. God was speaking to her in that moment as well. Nervously pacing around our kitchen, Becky frantically pointed out many of the questions with which I was also wrestling.

"Jim, how can you have an air ambulance service when you have no airplane and no money to buy one? How do you know there is truly a need for a charity air ambulance service? Who's going to fly the plane, assuming you can even get one? Who's going to provide medical care? And who's going to pay for all of this?"

I had no clue as to how to answer any of those very valid questions. But if God was truly calling Hal and Tami to begin this ministry, and I was convinced he was, I knew he would provide whatever was needed for the ministry to succeed so he would be glorified.

Experiencing God

A very common question asked by Christians is, "How can I know what God's will is for me?"

In considering the major decision Hal had placed before me, I reflected on the *Experiencing God* Bible study I had worked through a number of times. The author, Henry Blackaby, outlined a basic model of God's nature and how he relates to his people. Blackaby summarized his ideas in the following seven steps:

1. God is always at work around you.
2. God loves you in a real and intimate way.
3. God invites you to join him in his work.

4. God speaks by the Holy Spirit through prayer, the Bible, the church, and circumstances to reveal himself, his purposes, and his ways.
5. Following God will lead you to a crisis of belief, requiring faith and action.
6. You cannot stay where you are and follow God.
7. You come to know God better as you follow him and he reveals himself to you.

I believe most everyone, and certainly all who call themselves Christians, can accept the ideas that God is at work around them and he loves them intimately without much difficulty. And it is easy to acknowledge God invites *some* people to join him in his work, people such as pastors, evangelists, and missionaries. But life starts to get interesting when we recognize God is calling *every* believer to be obedient to his call to be involved in the work he is doing in the world.

Blackaby also believes God speaks to people in many different ways. I have evidence of him speaking into my life on many occasions. One specific instance comes to my mind—the time when I felt God calling me to go to Peru for the first time. As our church was seeking to adopt an unreached people group, God spoke through Pastor Dan McNerney to reveal to me we should partner with the church in Moyobamba, Peru, in sharing the gospel with the Aguaruna Indians.

Answering The Call

Hal had shared with me the vision God had given him for Grace on Wings. He had asked me to pray about serving as the medical director for this new venture. There was no doubt in my mind God was at work in Hal, and Hal had obediently answered God's call to start this new ministry. So for me, my decision to join with Hal and Tami and Gary in this new venture came down to one basic question. Would I obey God's call?

I prayed about it for several days, and I felt God assuring me it was the right choice for me. With tremendous excitement and a modicum of anxiety, I accepted Hal's invitation to volunteer the talents God had given me to serve as medical director for Grace on Wings. "All right, Hal," I said. "I'm in. I see God working here, so I can't refuse."

"Amen, brother! He's in charge, and I'm just his copilot" was his response.

In Genesis 12:1 the Lord said to Abram, "Leave your country, your people and your father's household and go to the land I will show you." Did Abram fully grasp all that was involved in saying yes to God? Probably not. It's a good thing God does not give us too much information when he calls us to action. If we knew all of the obstacles, struggles, and sacrifices that lay ahead, we would probably never leave our comfort zone.

Hal, Tami, Gary, and I were about to embark on a journey with the Lord, one step at a time, walking every step of the way on faith. We would soon learn just how costly this ministry would be.

Contrails Of Grace

In October 2006, Tami published the first newsletter, entitled *Contrails of Grace*, announcing the birth of Grace on Wings. The first issue described the heart of the mission, the reason why Grace on Wings was formed. She wrote, "In the beginning, we planned only a single mission, a trip to Peru with Dr. Milstead. The result was no less than God reaching down into our hearts and pulling out his plans for our future." Tami wrote about the people involved with the ministry and our need for volunteers, donors, and prayer warriors to support the ministry.

Contrails are the long thin clouds that sometimes form behind aircraft. They are visible signs of the path of a plane. *Contrails of Grace* similarly informs our followers of the path God has our ministry on by publishing reports and stories several times a year. The newsletter celebrates Grace on Wings' accomplishments, tells inspirational stories of the patients we serve, and makes known our needs to grow the ministry in order to share the love of Christ with those in need.

400 Ropes

Answering the call to this God-sized project was merely the first step in the formation of Grace on Wings. We knew we would need hundreds of volunteers, donors, and prayer warriors to partner with us to make the ministry successful. At the time, Hal estimated our fixed costs to operate the ministry each month at about $10,000. Our initial goal was to try to enlist four hundred people in giving $25 or more to cover the pre-flight costs. These "400 Ropes" members would receive a mission alert whenever we scheduled a flight. Their prayers would provide the spiritual fuel for our mission.

The biblical basis for the 400 Ropes program comes from Luke 5:17–26. In this portion of Scripture, Jesus attracts a large crowd as he is healing the sick. A paralytic is lowered through the roof of a house on his mat and placed right in front of Jesus. Jesus heals the paralytic because of the faith of his friends. Metaphorically, the 400 Ropes members are the friends placing our patients and our ministry before the Lord in prayer.

6

Attempt Great Things For God
("You Need How Much?")

Charles Spurgeon, the influential, nineteenth-century British Baptist preacher, wrote a sermon in 1888 entitled, "Is Anything Too Hard For The Lord?" In it he says, "Attempt great things for God. Attempt something which as yet you cannot do. Any fool can do what he can do. It is only the Believer who does what he cannot do. 'Is anything too hard for the Lord?' Fall back upon omnipotence and then go forward in the strength of it."

Hal, Tami, and I certainly were attempting something we could not do through our own efforts. So we prayed for wisdom and for God to bring the right people alongside us to establish Grace on Wings.

Climbing Mountains

Over the next few days, I remembered and thought about someone I had met the previous year who might be able to give us some advice and wisdom about how to proceed with plans for the ministry.

As I was sitting alone at a table in the reception area sipping coffee between sessions at a mission conference in Atlanta in 2005, Donna Thomas casually strolled by and introduced herself to me. She chose the chair next to me and began telling me about her extensive and exotic mission experiences dating back nearly fifty years. I discovered she and her husband had started their own non-profit mission organization many years before.

The significance of that meeting and what she shared held no importance to me at that time, as Grace on Wings would not even be conceived until the following year. But her next words did.

"If you want to learn more, you can read my book. It's called *Climb Another Mountain*, and it's for sale right over there on that bookstand by the checkout."

To my surprise, Donna then told me she lived in Carmel, Indiana, just forty miles from my home in Frankfort! I did buy Donna's book that day and subsequently read it with great interest.

Now, nearly a year later, I sensed how God had orchestrated my encounter with Donna. He knew Grace on Wings would one day benefit from her vast experience.

Hal had been invited to share his Peru mission trip experience with our church congregation during our annual Mission Sunday church service in early November of 2006. He took that opportunity to formally announce the birth of Grace on Wings to our congregation.

During lunch following the service, I told Hal and Tami about Donna Thomas and gave them her book to read. I said Donna lived on the north side of Indianapolis, and we should try to meet with her sometime soon. They agreed we should gain whatever knowledge we could from her experiences in order to avoid any pitfalls during our startup phase.

I phoned Donna later that same day and told her about Grace on Wings. She invited us to meet with her at her home to get to know each other better and see how she could help. She said she would also invite Pastor Pat Smith and his wife, Laura, to attend the meeting. Pastor Pat was serving as an Associate Pastor at Zionsville Presbyterian Church, where Donna worshiped.

In that instant I was awed by how God had been at work, bringing all of our lives together like an artisan skillfully weaving a beautiful tapestry. Pastor Pat and Laura Smith were the ones who had so diligently taught me how to study the Bible years before when they were leading the congregation at First Presbyterian Church in

Frankfort. They were the ones who had introduced me to mission work and had given me encouragement as I led the Mission Team. The news they would be at the upcoming meeting seemed like a confirmation from God that he was indeed leading this new venture, and it was our job to follow him in obedience.

Hal, Tami, Becky, and I met with Donna at her home in early November. Pastor Pat and Laura expressed their excitement as they heard Hal and Tami share the vision for Grace on Wings and how God had been at work in their lives. Then we listened intently as Donna gave her testimony about the nonprofit mission organization she and her husband, Chuck, had formed over forty years before.

Donna stressed how important it was to have a small board of directors who shared the same vision for Grace on Wings Hal and Tami had. She warned us we would have many "mountains to climb," but if we remained obedient to God's calling, he would always provide for our every need. At the end of the evening, Donna enthusiastically endorsed the vision for our new ministry and pledged to offer her support and advice whenever needed.

Taking Shape

A few weeks later, the first official board meeting for Grace on Wings was held on November 29, 2006. Hal, Tami, Pastor Gary Walker, and I met to discuss how to proceed in this exciting new endeavor. We realized we would need a few more board members, mature Christians with knowledge and expertise in business and finance, to complement the existing board.

Much time was spent praying for God to bring people with those talents and spiritual gifts to us. And then, with new confidence, we laid out a strategy for fundraising, recruiting volunteer pilots and medical personnel, and putting together material to present during speaking engagements to churches and civic organizations.

My first encounter with Pastor Gary Walker was at that initial board meeting. Immediately I could see why Hal and Tami had sought his advice and were eager to have him serve on the board of directors for Grace on Wings. He exhibited a very humble spirit while confidently giving godly direction to the efforts of our new ministry.

Pastor Gary told me he had first met Hal and Tami in 2005 at Grace Evangelical Church in Franklin during a class he was leading on spiritual gifts. The main Scripture he used for the lesson that day was 1 Peter 4:10 (paraphrased), "Each of you has received a gift to use to serve others. Be good servants of God's various gifts of grace." He knew Hal and Tami were going on a mission trip to Peru soon, so he challenged them to ask God how he wanted to use their gifts of aviation and medicine.

"Hal and Tami came back from Peru and told me the plans they had for ministry," Gary told me at that first board meeting. "I was so excited someone had actually listened to my teaching and applied it, so I had to say yes when they asked me to join them!"

I asked if he could see the hand of God at work in the formation of Grace on Wings.

"Oh, without a doubt," he said. "This is just crazy without God being involved!"

I laughed as I recalled my wife's recent, similar declaration, "Hal must be crazy!"

"I don't have any medical or aviation skills," said Pastor Gary. "I see my role as more of a friend, a pastor, and a board member. I feel called to do two things—be the gatekeeper of the ministry's vision, and keep Christ at the center of our mission."

Later I would learn Gary's story. He had been raised on a farm just south of Kirklin, Indiana, approximately thirty miles north of Indianapolis. His family had attended the Kirklin Presbyterian Church regularly, although he said their lives away from church showed little evidence of fruits of the Holy Spirit. But he did acquire a solid work ethic and wholesome virtues from his parents. His upbringing laid a solid foundation for the rest of his life.

Gary came to know Jesus as his Lord and Savior while in college at Ball State. He became very involved with The Navigators ministry and was discipled by them for almost three years. His last year at Ball State was spent with the Campus House ministry, which provided him the opportunity to lead worship, teach Bible studies, counsel other students, and clean toilets (he said he always thought of Jesus washing the disciples feet while doing this act of service).

Following college, Gary and his wife, Sharon, taught school for a number of years. Sharon eventually stayed home to raise their three children, while Gary moved from teaching to serving as the middle school principal at Heritage Christian School on the northeast side of Indianapolis. It was during those years that Gary received his call to pastoral ministry.

In 1990 Gary left his position at Heritage and attended Trinity Evangelical Divinity School in Deerfield, Illinois. Following seminary, he served as the pastor of family ministries at Valley Evangelical Free Church in Vacaville, California. After nine years, he and his family moved back to Indiana, and Gary began serving as the senior associate pastor at Grace Evangelical Church on the south side of Indianapolis. During his twelve years at Grace, he met Hal and Tami and began serving as the spiritual advisor to Grace on Wings. He later became the pastor of Connection Church of Franklin in Franklin, Indiana.

In parting that evening, Gary said to me, "God's in this. He wants it to flourish. We just have to be faithful and trust him each step of the journey."

As I left that first board meeting, I felt more at peace, knowing God had brought Gary to Grace on Wings. Gary would keep us centered spiritually by keeping our eyes firmly fixed on Jesus.

Expanding Our Board

Our next board meeting was held a few months later on February 8, 2007. That's when I was first introduced to Mike Meister and Roger Booth, our newest board members.

Mike Meister was employed as a technical pilot for the Rolls-Royce Corporation. He, like Hal, had a longstanding love affair with aviation. Mike had been praying about how to get involved in some sort of medical flight assist program, such as Angel Flights, before a friend told him about a new Christ-centered ministry called Grace on Wings.

He was immediately intrigued by the idea of using aviation and medicine as a vehicle to promote the gospel, so he called Hal and arranged a lunch meeting to learn more about this new opportunity.

"From that point on, I knew this was where God wanted me to serve," he told me.

Mike, like many other Christians, had been raised in a family that attended church out of practice rather than out of passion. "I recall I would pray the Lord's Prayer every night before going to bed, thinking that was good enough to be right with God," he said.

"Then one summer I attended a vacation Bible school, where the gospel was clearly explained to me. I realized, even at the age of nine, that I was a sinner. Nothing I could do through my own efforts—reciting prayers, being good, attending church—would make me right with God. Only belief in Jesus Christ, the Son of God, who died on the cross for my sins and rose again, could make me right with God. I prayed and asked Jesus to come into my heart. Even though I was still a child, I knew I was changed and needed to serve God."

Mike brought years of valuable experience in aviation and business to Grace on Wings. He provided Hal with the capable copilot needed to get our new ministry started. Mike's heart for the Lord and his passionate desire to serve were just what we needed to accomplish the God-sized mission we had all been called to.

Roger Booth, CPA and Director of Auditing for the State of Indiana, had been told by his close friend, Pastor Gary Walker, about the need for a solid Christian with an expertise in finance to join the board of Grace on Wings. Roger had previously served on many other boards and generally viewed them as a thankless opportunity. He could never really see that his participation had made a difference. When he learned about the mission of Grace on Wings, however, he was thrilled with the idea of serving as the Chief Financial Officer in a voluntary capacity.

Roger grew up in West Virginia and attended Marshall University, where he majored in business. He married after college and served in the Army Reserves. During his time in the Reserves, he began talking with his good friend Bill about spiritual matters.

One day, Roger told me, after Bill said something to him about Satan, he shot back, "Now wait a minute. I don't believe in Satan."

The next day Bill brought him a 3 x 5 index card with several Scripture verses written on it to show him exactly what the Bible had to say about Satan. Consistent with his deliberate and analytical nature, Roger delved into the Bible and began attending an evangelical church in order to learn the truth of God's Word for himself.

"That's when I realized I really wasn't a Christian. I'd never surrendered my life to Jesus," he said.

After college he moved to Indiana, where he cultivated a very successful career as a certified public accountant. As he matured spiritually, he learned to "pray big" because "the God we serve wants us to do big things for others." Even after hearing about the huge financial startup costs facing Grace on Wings, Roger was at peace as he made the decision to join our board. In contrast to his customary conservative business practices, he believed the Lord would provide all we needed to make the new ministry succeed.

Our board of directors was then complete. We knew each of us had been given certain spiritual gifts and talents to use to accomplish the challenging work ahead. God had been preparing us, skillfully shaping each of our lives like a potter molding the clay in his hands to create a beautiful work of art. We believed Grace on Wings would indeed become a thing of beauty, but our focus needed to be continually on the Creator, the one true living God.

God's Order of Events

Hal had been researching the air ambulance industry for over seven months and had decided the ideal plane for our ministry was the MU-2. He was very familiar with this aircraft, as he had flown it extensively during the time he was flying cargo on the East Coast in the early 1990s.

The MU-2 had a bad reputation in the aviation industry as a result of an inordinate amount of aircraft accidents. Hal knew those mishaps occurred because of poorly trained pilots flying beyond their limitations and not because of inherent problems with the aircraft. He also knew some MU-2s had previously been used as air ambulances with great success.

Hal recalled meeting a pilot at the Greenwood Airport just south of Indianapolis who owned an MU-2. When Hal shared his vision for the formation of Grace on Wings, the pilot said he would consider selling his MU-2 to our new organization. Hal made contact with the pilot again. When he offered to sell his plane to us, our newly formed board was faced with the first of many major decisions. The asking price of the plane was more than our meager budget could afford. In addition, his MU-2 was a short body style, which was smaller than what we needed to get patients in and out of the aircraft safely and efficiently.

Hal made an impassioned plea to the board to purchase the plane, and he even offered to put his personal finances on the line to accomplish this. After much prayer, however, the wisdom of the board compelled us to wait on the Lord to provide the right aircraft at a better price that would not place such a strain on our new ministry.

Psalm 27:14 says, "Wait for the LORD; be strong and take heart and wait for the LORD." We waited and trusted the Lord to provide the right plane for us, and within a few months we would see him provide for us according to his order of events in ways we could not have anticipated.

As Hal and Tami searched the Internet for charity or faith-based air ambulance services, they came across an organization called Mercy Med Flight based in Ft. Worth, Texas. Hal contacted the organization and discovered that Mercy Med Flight went out of business about the time Grace on Wings was conceived. Mercy Med Flight had reportedly gotten away from its faith-based ministry and lost the support from its conservative backers. Then, when expensive mechanical problems left the leadership deeply in debt, they decided to cease operations.

"It was like God just removed their lamp stand and passed it on to us," Hal said.

From Mercy Med Flight's experience, we learned a valuable lesson. We vowed never to chase the almighty dollar but remain committed to our original mission, showing the love of Christ through aviation.

Even though we still had no plane for the ministry, Hal realized we would eventually need a specialized cot system, or stretcher, for whatever aircraft we subsequently used as an air ambulance. He made multiple inquiries into the procurement of a new or used cot system. He was shocked to learn a new customized cot system would cost nearly $100,000!

At that time such a purchase was inconceivable, as we had only received a small amount in donations. Fortunately, Hal located a used cot system, valued at $24,000, which was owned by an individual in Tennessee. By divine intervention, Hal was able to negotiate a reduced price, and we obtained the cot system for only $10,000! Board member Roger Booth graciously donated the full amount needed to purchase the cot.

In May of 2007, Hal had to attend an annual orthopedics conference in St. Louis, Missouri. As he was walking through the area where vendors were exhibiting their products, he saw the Clint Pharmaceuticals booth. His gaze fixed on a small, blue paperback book that looked like a PDR (Physician's Desk Reference). But when he picked up the book, he discovered the title was actually *Physician's Life Reference*. It contained information not about medications but the New Testament, Psalms, and Proverbs.

Hal immediately knew it was perfect for giving to each patient we served through Grace on Wings. He introduced himself to the Clint Pharmaceutical representative. Hal explained the ministry of Grace on Wings and how he wanted to give the *Physician's Life Reference* to our patients and anyone else who wanted to read God's Word.

The representative told Hal the book helped medical professionals be prepared to treat more than just pain by giving patients practical solutions to life's challenges. He pledged to donate a large number to our new ministry.

A valuable relationship was formed that day. Since then, Grace on Wings has had the privilege of passing out thousands of these Bibles during our annual Hog Roast, Gala, air shows, and other events.

An Essential Partnership

Hal had been searching continuously for an MU-2 by poring over aircraft trade journal advertisements and contacting aircraft brokers. As a board, we had tentatively set an upper limit of $250,000 for the purchase price of an airplane. Since several large banks in the Indianapolis area had reviewed our ministry plans and rejected our requests for a loan to purchase an aircraft, we were praying that someone would be willing to donate an aircraft or take a tax write-off for a substantial portion of the value of the plane. But even with such a donation, where would we get the rest of the financial backing we needed to get the ministry started?

I had been banking at The Farmers Bank in Frankfort, Indiana, for over seventeen years at that time. Just months before, I had met with Karen Miller, the bank's president, to see if the bank might make a charitable donation to our new organization. Karen explained that The Farmers Bank only donated to local charities in Frankfort and Clinton Counties. A donation to Grace on Wings, therefore, was not within the scope of the bank's mission since we were based in Indianapolis.

I urged Hal to talk with The Farmers Bank in Frankfort about a loan. Hal called the bank and spoke with Karen Miller. She agreed to set up an appointment for Hal and me to meet with her and several of the loan officers at the bank.

When the day of the meeting arrived, Hal gave a passionate presentation outlining the vision and mission of Grace on Wings. Karen and her cohorts had heard many loan requests before, but they knew this one was different. They asked us many of the same questions we had been asking ourselves for nearly a year. What would our operating costs be? How would we generate revenue? What other capital expenditures did we expect to incur? How many employees would we have?

Hal explained we were an all-volunteer organization and would have no employees. We did have some projections as to what our operating expenses and revenue stream might look like. Everyone present knew, however, all our plans were based solely on faith.

We were relying on faith that God would send us the patients who needed our service. Faith donors would come alongside us to help cover our expenses. And faith volunteers would continually sacrifice their free time to provide the manpower needed to sustain the ministry.

After some deliberation, Karen and her associates said they liked what we intended to do and wanted to partner with Grace on Wings by loaning us the $250,000 to purchase a plane.

"Praise God!" Hal said, overcome with joy.

When we left the bank, Hal and I high-fived and then poured out prayers of thanksgiving to God for providing the financial backing we needed to get the ministry off the ground, literally and figuratively.

Once again we had just witnessed God at work. From a worldly perspective, the plans we had were shaky at best. But God's Word gave us assurance he would supply whatever we needed to make Grace on Wings succeed. We claimed Philippians 1:6, "Being confident of this, that he who began a good work in you will carry it on to completion until the day of Christ Jesus."

I admit, there were times in the beginning when we became discouraged and considered just using our own finances to rush out and buy a plane. But had we done so, we would not have had the opportunity to see God receive the glory for making provision for us.

We learned a valuable lesson that day about the way in which God works. Psalm 27:14 says, "Wait for the LORD; be strong and take heart and wait for the LORD." Waiting for God to provide for our needs went against our human desire to make things happen in our way and according to our timing. But the rewards for doing so were indeed heavenly!

7

Experiencing God's Blessings
("Whoa, Nellie!")

After obtaining financing from The Farmers Bank, Hal intensified his search for a plane. An aircraft broker called him one day and said he had located an MU-2 for sale, but the owner was asking $405,000. Hal got the tail number of the aircraft, N910NF, and researched the plane online. He liked what he saw.

Knowing the asking price was more than the board had approved, Hal told the broker to offer the owner $250,000 and a charitable tax deduction for the remainder of the market value of the plane. Hal said to explain to the owner that we were a nonprofit organization and would be using the plane as an air ambulance.

A short time later Hal received a call from the broker who said, "Your offer was accepted."

"Praise God!" Hal replied. "Now tell me what's wrong with this airplane!"

The broker told Hal he could contact the owner of the aircraft and discuss further details with him. Hal got the phone number and called the owner. He immediately sensed that the voice on the other end of the line was familiar. To Hal's surprise, the owner said he lived in Carmel, Indiana, and had not one but three MU-2s that he used for business purposes.

As they were talking further about the plane, the owner, Greg Mink, said suddenly, "Hal, is that you?"

"Absolutely!" Hal replied, confirming what he already knew.

Through divine intervention, Hal and Greg had met each other briefly several years before when Hal had operated on Greg's son. They had enthusiastically discussed MU-2s at that time because the fraternity of MU-2 pilots was fairly small and tight-knit. Hal related the unfolding story of Grace on Wings to Greg and was relieved to learn there were no major problems with the aircraft. Greg pledged his support of our new endeavor and promised to help in any way he could.

When Hal called me and told me what happened, we both knew we had witnessed God at work once again. Just as Blackaby had said, "You come to know God better as you follow him and he reveals himself to you." We were indeed coming to know God better as we saw how he was providing for our every need in ways we could not even imagine.

The obstacles we faced in starting and maintaining Grace on Wings were all God-sized problems. But that is where we all can most clearly see God at work. When we don't attempt anything beyond what we can do through our own efforts, we won't experience the blessing of God revealing himself to us.

Caveats and Blessings

At least two major caveats remained to the story of finding our plane and preparing it for flight. First, according to FAA regulations, an aircraft's engines have to be completely overhauled or replaced after six thousand hours of flight time. And our MU-2 only had six hundred hours of flight time left on each engine before we could no longer fly. The cost of two new engines would be approximately $600,000!

Hal had estimated that we might be able to fly for two to three years before facing this major expenditure. We didn't know how God would provide the funding we needed, but we were certain that he was not caught by surprise or in awe of the expense. So we decided to move ahead, trusting that when the time came for new engines for the plane, God would make it happen.

At this point, we had located a plane but still did not have the funds to purchase it. We were in the process of supplying The Farmers Bank with the financial information necessary to process and obtain our loan. Meanwhile, the aircraft broker informed us we needed to pay $10,000 in earnest money immediately in order to secure the plane under the terms we had discussed.

As an elder in my church, the First Presbyterian Church in Frankfort, I was aware that a deceased former member, Nell Wood, had bequeathed some money to the church to be used at the discretion of the Session. On May 16, 2007, I sent an email to my pastor describing our urgent need for $10,000 to secure the plane for Grace on Wings. He and many of the Session members were aware of the existence of Grace of Wings and our initial efforts to begin the ministry. He promised to address the issue at our scheduled Session meeting that night.

At the meeting, I related to the Session the need we had. One of the Session members, Jack Ransom, made a motion to donate $10,000 to Grace on Wings from the Nell Wood bequest with the stipulation that her name would be inscribed on the plane. That motion was seconded and unanimously approved. Following the Session meeting, I immediately phoned Hal and told him we not only had the $10,000 but we also had a name for our plane—"Nellie."

A second caveat was preparing the plane for flight. Following the purchase of Nellie, it became apparent we would need to make some modifications and improvements in the plane's navigation and electrical systems according to Hal's specifications. Nellie was housed at Intercontinental Jet Services (ICJ) in Tulsa, Oklahoma, at the time we acquired her. Hal knew ICJ was the maintenance center for MU-2s nationally, so he made arrangements for the desired changes in Nellie to be made there just prior to the start of our ministry.

The administrators at ICJ were extremely excited about Grace on Wings. They pledged to perform maintenance on Nellie at a reduced rate as a charitable contribution to the ministry. Even then, the maintenance bill was estimated at approximately $50,000.

So, before the ink was dry on our initial loan with The Farmers Bank, Hal called and apologetically asked the loan officer, Kendra, if we could increase the amount of the loan from $250,000 to $300,000.

"What's $50,000 between friends," she said. "I'll see what I can do!"

The bank did supply the $300,000 we needed to get Nellie ready for her first mission, something still somewhere over the distant horizon. But at least we already had climbed some of the mountains we would face in the start-up, and we had learned to trust in God along the way.

Final Details Before First Flight

With start-up details out of the way, we were ready to focus on the reason for the creation of Grace on Wings and get going with it. The initial mission focus was to target patients who were medically stable and would not require any medications or advanced life support treatment during flight. These patients were typically ones who had suffered an illness or injury far from their home or their family and were in need of transport from one medical facility to another. Our patients would be those who were unable to tolerate a commercial flight or a long transport by ground ambulance.

Although others had assured us the need for such a charity air ambulance service was huge, we still did not know how great the demand would be. But we did know whatever service we provided must be worthy of the calling we had received so God would be glorified.

To that end, Hal insisted we go before the Indiana State EMS Commission and obtain their official approval for our unique ministry. Having served as the Clinton County EMS Medical Director for many years, I was able to establish the medical protocols we would need to submit to the EMS Commission for review.

As part of the process, Hal and I also met with two prominent emergency medicine specialists from Indianapolis who served on the board of the Indiana State EMS Commission. They were very intrigued with our ministry and said that, although there was no requirement for Grace on Wings to receive the approval of the EMS

Commission, such an effort on our part would be well received. We were invited to make a presentation to the full board at their next meeting on November 16, 2007.

In order to advertise our new ministry and raise new supporters, Hal and Tami had been busy planning a hog roast fundraising event at the Greenwood Airport. The event was scheduled for September 15, 2007. Meanwhile, Nellie was still in Tulsa, Oklahoma, getting the maintenance she needed. There was no certainty she would be ready to be displayed at the hog roast. After much prayer and extensive maintenance, Nellie was finally flown to Indianapolis from Tulsa the day before the hog roast, much to Hal's relief.

Hal would later say, "Up until the night before I flew Nellie home for the first time, I wasn't too worried. But as I lay in bed that particular night, it suddenly hit me this was for real. I began to think about all of the things that could go wrong and all the ways we could fail.

"The enormity of what we were about to do almost overwhelmed me. The only thing I could do was to turn it over to God. I said, 'Lord, you called me to this mission, and I am trusting you to provide for us day by day. We can't do this in our own power.'" Only then did Hal sense the peace of God, and he was able to drift off to sleep.

Hal had been storing the used cot system, purchased nearly six months before, in the garage at his home. Now that Nellie and the cot were both in the same place, he wanted to see if the two would be compatible. To his amazement, the cot system fit perfectly. When power was applied to the system, everything operated without a flaw. It was only later Hal discovered that the very same cot system he had purchased in Tennessee had been used in Nellie when she had functioned as an air ambulance in Traverse City, Michigan, years before!

All he could say was, "Praise God! He knew what we would be needing long before we did." Time and time again God continually provided spiritual markers for us to see him at work.

The hog roast was well attended and gave us our first opportunity to show Nellie to the public. In order to formally commission the plane for the mission she would perform, Pastor Gary Walker urged everyone in attendance to gather around the aircraft and lay hands on Nellie as he led in prayer.

A few months later, on November 16, 2007, Hal stood before the Indiana State EMS Commission and explained the scope of the medical aviation ministry we were hoping to begin. He asked that Grace on Wings be given a waiver from the existing rules, which classified an air ambulance as an ALS (advanced life support) service. Since we were seeking only a BLS (basic life support) certification at that time, the waiver was necessary.

The board unanimously approved the waiver, gave us their approval, and then applauded! One board member, himself a pilot, even said he would fly with us anytime we needed.

Now we had everything we needed to begin our ministry— except a patient.

Prepare For Takeoff

Tami was still working full-time as an ER physician assistant during the fall of 2007 as we were eagerly waiting for our initial flight request to come in. She was in charge of assembling a list of volunteer EMTs, paramedics, and nurses to staff each flight and ascertain that every volunteer received the necessary training for our air ambulance work.

Once again, one of our major fears was allayed. We had many highly trained volunteers offer their time and talents to the ministry. Most of these volunteers were working full-time in the medical field, but they felt compelled to volunteer with Grace on Wings because they desired to share the love of Jesus with our patients.

Hal had been compiling a list of copilots who had volunteered to fly in the right seat of Nellie. And an official Grace on Wings website had been launched. Were we ready at last for takeoff?

A few people had called to inquire about our ministry, but our first official flight request would be triggered by a front-page news article printed in the Thanksgiving Day edition of the *Indianapolis Star*. That first mission to serve Carlos Escobar was quickly followed by a second flight, and then a third. The requests increased steadily as more and more people became aware of our ministry.

James' Story

We flew James from Denver, Colorado, to Tampa, Florida. Tami wrote this account when we answered the call to serve him.

James' family had been working with us for over two months to try and get him back to Tampa, Florida, where they lived. He had been alone for months in a Denver hospital with only an occasional visit from his family. He was suffering from kidney and liver failure, which resulted in cardiac arrest several times. He was resuscitated each time but remained very unstable.

I told his son, Joe, we would have to change his status to "Do Not Resuscitate" to be able to fly him home. I explained this didn't mean we wouldn't treat him. It only meant we wouldn't do CPR or land if he became unstable. We'd have to rely on God to keep him safe during the flight.

James was asked to sign a statement to this effect and eagerly said, "If that's what gets me home, I'll sign it."

Tami told me later, "As we loaded him onto the plane, I gave Hal a look that said 'this guy's really sick.' After James was prayed over and secured in the plane, I called you for advice.

"Chris, the respiratory therapist, and I worked hard to stabilize him. As I was reading through his hospital records, I discovered he had actually died earlier that day before we arrived to transfer him. But God is good and James was relatively stable with medication during our five and a half-hour flight.

"When we finally landed in Tampa, James said, 'I made it home!'

"We were met by his family at the VA hospital. My heart always jumps when I see a family finally reunited. His daughter, Jamie, and son, Joe, were there with hugs and tears to greet him. They were given a copy of the Bible and stayed by his side while we prayed with James before we left.

"I learned that James died a few days later. The family called and said they were so happy to have had a few good days with him—his last days on earth.

"As I reflect back on our ministry, I realize many of our patients have died. It's then that I love our motto: 'What does it matter if you transport someone and give them an extra year or two of life if you don't introduce them to the One who gives eternal life?'"

God At Work

We don't always know all the ways God uses Grace on Wings to impact the lives of others. But we do know he is at work, often in ways we don't anticipate. This truth is apparent in the following testimony from Kendra Price, Commercial Loan Officer at The Farmers Bank.

Hal Blank, CEO and Chief Pilot, has always said that Grace on Wings (GOW) began on a "wing and a prayer," but without the solid team GOW built to begin this ministry, their ability to see it grow and prosper would not have been possible. Initially, in the eyes of a bank, this was another start-up company. We liked their idea, but it was their sound business plan and realistic projections that gave The Farmers Bank the confidence to get involved.

Overall this has been a great relationship with a very well run company. We were excited for them when Nellie, their first air ambulance got her new engines, and Abe, the most recent aircraft was added to the fleet. I have become passionate about their mission and support them not only as their loan officer but personally as well. I look forward to our ongoing relationship as we continue to do our small part in their very large mission of "showing God's love through aviation."

Thanks for the opportunity to express why the bank believes in GOW.

8

Leaving A Legacy
("The Gift That Keeps On Giving")

Not long after our first flight with Carlos Escobar, we were called upon to transport a woman from nearby Lafayette in need of medical care at a hospital in Indianapolis and then a woman from Iowa needing transport to Virginia. We were ready for our next challenge.

The ministry of Grace on Wings was in full swing by that time, having had several opportunities to serve and some amazing stories to tell. Each one is carefully documented, but the details are kept confidential for multiple reasons. Some patients or their family members, however, are very excited to have us share their stories publicly. Sister Hildegarde's family was one of those who wanted her story to be told.

Sister Hildegarde's Story

In January of 2008, Sister Hildegarde Smith, an 83-year-old nun, suffered a massive stroke while performing charity work in Cimarron, New Mexico. The stroke left her paralyzed on the right side of her body and unable to speak or walk. She was subsequently hospitalized at the Swedish Medical Center in Denver, Colorado, where she was bedridden and unable to perform any of the usual activities of daily living.

When a crisis and need such as in this case arises, the hospital case manager or a family member explores a number of transportation options to arrange a safe transfer in the most cost-effective manner. Often they contact a for-profit air ambulance service and receive a quote. Sticker shock sets in as the price for a commercial air ambulance flight is often beyond the reach of most people. That's when those in need turn to Grace on Wings for help.

Hal initially receives all calls from people requesting transport of a patient. As the chief pilot on every mission, he is best able to determine whether Grace on Wings can perform the requested transfer safely and efficiently. He has to consider a number of factors—distance of the transport, available airports nearby, weight of patient and passengers, weather conditions, and others. Then he can determine the cost of a flight and communicate this information to the patient's family or hospital case manager. Hal then refers them to Tami to coordinate further details.

Tami obtains patient medical information from the sending hospital and speaks with the hospital case manager. She then forwards the patient's medical records to me. As Medical Director for the ministry, I must decide if the patient is stable for the proposed transport. If so, Tami makes arrangements with the patient's family, ground ambulance transport services, and the receiving facility. Finally, she contacts volunteer medical personnel—nurses, paramedics, or respiratory therapists—to staff the proposed mission.

Many times patients and their families cannot afford the expense of an air ambulance flight, even a charity flight like Grace on Wings provides. In such cases, Hal and Tami offer advice about obtaining charitable donations from churches, civic groups, or individuals to cover the cost of the mission.

In this case, Paul Smith, brother of Sister Hildegarde, initially sent an email to Angel Flight to seek help in transporting her from Denver to Chicago. Angel Flight is a nonprofit charitable organization of pilots who voluntarily fly ambulatory patients who do not require any medical care during the flight. The personnel at Angel Flight recognized this patient did not meet their mission profile, as she was not ambulatory and would need medical care during the transport. Angel Flight referred Paul to Grace on Wings, and Paul contacted Hal by email through our website.

Paul's email described Sister Hildegarde's situation and her need. He also mentioned she had taught school in the Midwest for forty-nine years before transitioning to mission work in Cimarron, New Mexico. There she had served for fourteen years until she suffered the stroke.

"We are hoping to find a way to transport Sister Hildegarde from Denver to Chicago, where the order has their headquarters and a skilled nursing center for aged and disabled nuns," the email said. "She is by herself in Denver and needs people surrounding her whom she knows. In addition to her religious family in Chicago, her biological family live in Indiana and Michigan, all within a few hour's drive of Chicago."

In support of the pending transfer, a social worker at The Swedish Medical Center in Denver wrote, "Sister Smith would certainly benefit from the generous services of Grace on Wings, as there is currently no alternative method of transporting her home."

After reading Paul's email, Hal called and assured him Grace on Wings could help. Hal and Tami then began the necessary preparations for the mission.

Sister Hildegarde's situation was one we would see played out over and over again as our ministry advanced. A medical crisis — heart attack, stroke, motor vehicle accident, severe infection — would unexpectedly render a person helpless and alone, often thousands of miles from family and other support groups. In addition, most would have no insurance coverage for transport and very limited resources for paying for such a transport on their own.

For this mission, the Grace on Wings crew would have to fly from Indianapolis to Denver the day before the scheduled transport because of the distance involved and the bad weather they were facing. Hal arranged for Nellie to be kept in a hangar at the Denver airport overnight while the crew was lodged at a nearby hotel. He prepared a flight plan and carefully checked the weather forecast along the flight path. Tami arranged to visit Sister Hildegarde at the hospital and made sure she was ready for the transfer.

The weather in Denver on the day of the transport was characteristically cold and windy, but with only a sprinkling of snow on the ground. The local Denver TV stations had picked up on Sister Hildegarde's compelling story, and their crews were on site to document preflight activities. Two nuns were there to make the journey to Chicago with Sister Hildegarde in order to provide prayer and emotional support during the difficult time in her life. It was fitting that one who had given her whole life serving others should now be comforted by those who shared her love for the Lord.

During the flight to Chicago, the weather deteriorated dramatically as the crew and passengers proceeded eastward from Denver. By the time Hal was ready to make the approach into the Palwaukee Airport, a blowing snowstorm was raging through the Chicago area, lowering visibility to near zero. Hal was concerned the airport might be closed before he could get the plane safely on the ground. He always had a backup plan prepared to land at an alternate airport in case weather conditions made it unsafe to land at the intended destination.

"Man, this is bad!" Hal said to the crew as they descended through the blinding snowstorm in search of the runway below. "Tami, make sure everyone is buckled up back there. It's going to get rough on the way down."

Blinded by the snow, Hal relied on the aircraft's instruments for navigation while being brutally buffeted around by the powerful gusts of wind. Nellie finally broke through the clouds about 500 feet above the ground, revealing runway lights barely visible through a ghostly haze. With every muscle in his body tensed for action, Hal caught sight of the Palwaukee Airport at the last moment and landed Nellie on its snow-covered runway.

Once on the ground, Hal breathed a sigh of relief and taxied to his designated parking spot. When the crew opened the door to the aircraft, they saw before them a large assembly of nuns and the Mother Superior of the convent standing on the tarmac in the blinding snowstorm, waiting to welcome Sister Hildegarde home!

"We've been praying for you," Mother Superior told Hal.

"Amen, Sister. We needed it!" he replied.

Sister Hildegarde was transported from the airport to the convent, where she would live out her final days surrounded by the loving members of her convent. When God called Sister Hildegarde home to be with him in heaven three months later, all of her family traveled to Chicago for the funeral.

A member of Sister Hildegarde's convent, Caroline Schafer, wrote us a note and shared the following:

> On the coldest, windiest day of the year, we met this little plane with the cross on its tail at a small airport north of Chicago. There were three of us Sisters there, and each of us had to fight tears when Sister Hildegard was so tenderly and lovingly transferred from Nellie to the stretcher for her ride in Superior Ambulance to the nursing home. I followed the ambulance to the nursing home and was so very grateful to the crew of Grace On Wings for having accompanied Sister, making sure she was safely in her bed. All of you who work with Grace On Wings are remembered frequently in my prayer. God bless you and keep you and your families close to Him.

Celebrating A Relationship

Hal and Tami had hoped to attend the funeral. Grace on Wings, however, was carrying out another mission that day. So Hal contacted Paul Smith and informed him that he and Tami were having a cookout at their home the weekend following the funeral. He invited Paul and the rest of his family members to visit Indianapolis and celebrate Sister Hildegarde's life by sharing time together at the cookout.

Paul and a number of his family accepted the invitation. They had a wonderful time, sharing fond memories of Sister Hildegarde's life and learning more about the ministry of Grace on Wings and the people behind it. As a result, a lasting relationship would develop between Paul and Hal and other family members.

On the day of the cookout, Paul told Hal he had been making a monthly donation to Sister Hildegarde's convent for years to help support her work. "I'll give that money to Grace on Wings for as long as I'm able," he told Hal.

Paul has been a faithful supporter for over six years now. Sister Hildegarde's extended family also has continued to support the ministry. Additionally, Grace on Wings has received a donation from Sister Hildegarde's convent each year on the anniversary of her transport from Denver to Chicago. What a legacy Sister Hildegarde has left for our ministry and all of the people we serve!

Where Is Our Treasure?

As I reflected on Sister Hildegarde's story, the impact of her life of service to others, and the response of her family after her passing, I was challenged to discern what my legacy might be.

Sooner or later, all of us need to ask ourselves what we will leave behind when our life here on earth comes to an end. Do we, like Hal and Tami, want to leave a spiritual legacy of sharing the love of Jesus with others by using our time, talents, and treasures to help those in need? I know I do.

When we pass, will family members know without a doubt we have a home in heaven and will live forever in the presence of God? Or will they mourn in doubt, never having heard us publicly acknowledge Jesus as Lord and Savior? And will the treasures we hold in our hands be passed on in ways that will bless and help others in need, or will they pass on to others in a way that does not further God's kingdom here on earth?

It may be tempting to believe that someday, when we get life squared away according to our own desires and timetable, we'll fully commit to Jesus as Savior and Lord and make our treasures a gift that keeps on giving. As an ER doctor, however, I see lives unexpectedly and tragically altered or ended every single day. I mourn for those who risk an eternity apart from God and those who have no vision for sharing the things of this world they hold onto, which do not last.

About ten years ago, I read a fantastic book by Randy Alcorn entitled, *The Treasure Principle: Discovering the Secret of Joyful Giving.* In this book, the author points out that 15 percent of

everything Christ said in the Bible relates to money and possessions—more than his teachings on heaven and hell combined. Why?
Because our approach to money and possessions is central to our
spiritual lives.

One of Jesus' most neglected teachings, and the foundation for
the Treasure Principle, comes from Matthew 6.

> Do not store up for yourselves treasures on earth, where
> moth and rust destroy, and where thieves break in and steal.
> But store up for yourselves treasures in heaven, where moth
> and rust do not destroy, and where thieves do not break in
> and steal. For where your treasure is, there your heart will be
> also. (Matthew 6:19–21)

When we die, we take nothing with us. Our physical treasures
become someone else's. But how can we store up another kind of
treasure, the kind that remains forever? By serving God and others
with our time, talents, and monetary resources during our time here
on this earth.

Perhaps Jim Elliot, the Christian missionary killed in 1956
while attempting to evangelize the Auca Indians in Ecuador, said it
best. "He is no fool who gives what he cannot keep to gain what he
cannot lose."

What about retirement? Shouldn't Christians be able to enjoy life
during their last years here on earth? Absolutely! But for a Christian,
the kind of enjoyment that will bring total fulfillment means more
than the typical American dream of retirement.

John Piper points out a similar thought in his book, *Getting Old
for the Glory of God*.

> If we are going to make God look glorious in the last years
> of our lives, we must be satisfied in him. He must be our
> Treasure. And the life that we live must flow from this
> all-satisfying Christ. And the life that flows from the soul
> that lives on Jesus is a life of love and service. This is what
> will make Christ look great. When our hearts find their rest

in Christ, we stop using other people to meet our needs, and instead we make ourselves servants to meet their needs.

Sister Hildegarde did indeed grow old for the glory of God. She was still serving others as a missionary at age eighty-three. She knew heaven, not earth, was her home. And she knew the only things she would take with her when she left this world were spiritual in nature, not material.

Do we all have to be "missionaries" until our last breath is taken in order to have lived a meaningful life? Yes and no. As followers of Jesus, we are all called to go and make disciples. But answering that call may mean reaching out to people in need right in our own communities, perhaps even right in our own families. The apostle Paul stated the principle well.

Command those who are rich in this present world not to be arrogant nor to put their hope in wealth, which is so uncertain, but to put their hope in God, who richly provides us with everything for our enjoyment. Command them to do good, to be rich in good deeds, and to be generous and willing to share. In this way they will lay up treasure for themselves as a firm foundation for the coming age, so that they may take hold of the life that is truly life. (1 Timothy 6:17–19)

The ministry of Grace on Wings is totally dependent on donations—time, talents, and treasures—from people who are generous and willing to share. What makes Grace on Wings unique as an air ambulance service? The goal of our ministry is to provide high-quality medical care while also addressing the spiritual needs of our patients and their loved ones. We invite all who hear and are blessed or challenged by our mission to join us in ministry and give gifts that keep on giving!

9

Knowing and Serving God Better
("An Invitation To The Feast")

Every two years Mitsubishi holds a series of PROP (Pilot's Review of Proficiency) meetings at various locations around the United States. These meetings are held to inform MU-2 owners and pilots about any relevant changes or improvements that have taken place in the aviation industry.

Hal was invited by Mitsubishi to speak about Grace on Wings at all three PROP meetings during 2008, just a few months after we had begun flying. Mitsubishi was very supportive of our use of the MU-2 as a charity air ambulance and was eager to dispel the rumor that their aircraft was unsafe.

Hal knew the PROP meetings were a secular event and many in attendance might not agree with his words that would bring Jesus into their midst. He also realized, however, what he had been called to do—to show the love of Christ through aviation, whether on the ground or in the air. So, after much prayer, he faithfully presented the mission of Grace on Wings at the first meeting and, after thanking our corporate partners Mitsubishi and Honeywell, gave all of the glory to God.

The Grace on Wings Board of Directors had determined at the outset we could never compromise our ministry by excluding our faith. We knew if we ever accepted donations from someone who asked us to abstain from mentioning God, "tone down" our talk about Jesus, or remove the prominent red cross from Nellie's tail, God would remove his blessings from our ministry. At the same time, we were hopeful that Mitsubishi, our MU-2 manufacturer, and Honeywell, the manufacturer of our engines, would somehow help us obtain new engines for Nellie in the not-too-distant future. The relationships Hal developed would bear fruit for our ministry just a few years later.

Casey's Story

By May of 2008, we had flown eleven missions. It was then a request was made for Grace on Wings to transport a patient all the way from Shelbyville, Indiana, to Seattle, Washington—a distance of more than two thousand miles. The patient, a teenager named Casey, had been residing in a specialized long-term care facility for children. He had been separated from his family for over a year.

Casey's story began in 2006. His father was working in Indiana when Casey and his family came to the Hoosier state from Seattle for a visit. During this visit, 17-year-old Casey suffered a seizure lasting more than fifteen hours. Despite heroic treatment, he sustained severe brain damage that left him on a ventilator and totally dependent on specially trained providers for all of his daily needs.

Soon thereafter, Casey's family had to return to Seattle. But the cost of transporting Casey on a for-profit air ambulance was quoted as $30,000, and it would not be covered by insurance. Lacking the means to pay for the transfer, Casey's family was forced to make the agonizing decision to leave Casey in the long-term care facility in Indiana while they went back to their home in Seattle, Washington.

Casey's mother had a note put on the front of Casey's medical chart that said, "Don't tell him we had to go back to Seattle."

Tami learned of Casey's tragic situation from medical colleagues in the Shelbyville area. She felt compelled to offer the assistance of Grace on Wings. She subsequently visited Casey and discussed his case with the medical staff and with his family. When Casey's father's employer learned of the dilemma, he generously donated the $15,000 Grace on Wings needed to cover our cost of transporting Casey back to Seattle, where he would be near his family once again.

Some twenty months after Casey came to Indiana, Grace on Wings made a seven-hour flight in Nellie to take him back to Seattle. The news story was so compelling the Indianapolis NBC affiliate, WTHR, covered the flight by sending a news reporter and cameraman on the flight with the Grace on Wings crew.

"When we landed in Seattle," Hal said, "the family literally ran out to meet the airplane. Casey needed to be with his family. Can you imagine having to leave your loved one behind like that?"

As the door of the plane was opened, Casey's father said, "When I saw the plane coming down out of the clouds, I thanked God in heaven for returning my son to me."

The five-minute WTHR-13 news video from this flight can be seen on our website at www.graceonwings.org.

New Credentials

From the inception of our ministry, Hal knew it would be very important for Grace on Wings to be an active member of the professional organizations that governed the air ambulance industry. We were a small, nonprofit organization operating in an industry dominated by large hospital programs and for-profit corporations. In order to have the professional credential, therefore, Grace on Wings became a member of the Association of Air Medical Services (AAMS). For the same reason, I became a member of the Air Medical Physician Association (AMPA).

Next we learned that every October an Air Medical Transport Conference (AMTC) brought together medical aviation personnel from throughout the United States and around the world for the purpose of providing continuing education and industry updates. So Hal, Tami, our chief paramedic Eric Frantz, and I attended the 2008 AMTC event in Minneapolis, Minnesota.

Not only was Grace on Wings the only charity air ambulance with representatives present, but we also were the only faith-based volunteer organization represented. Most of the people we met were involved in rotary wing (helicopter) programs run by a large hospital or a fixed-wing, for-profit corporation flying Lear jets. Nevertheless, the educational sessions were very interesting and pertinent to what we hoped to become, an advanced life support (ALS) air ambulance equipped to transport all patients.

By the end of our first year of operations, we had flown an amazing twenty-seven missions. For every request that fit our mission profile, however, we turned down several others. Those requests were for patients who were much sicker and required ALS care. We were not yet prepared to handle patients requiring ventilator support, IV medications, and specialized critical care nursing skills.

Hundreds of vendors exhibited their medical aviation products and services in the cavernous convention center throughout the week of AMTC activities. One day we saw an exhibit displaying new customized Med-Pac cot systems. We stopped to talk with the man behind the exhibit, Ralph Braaten. Ralph lived in Minnesota and more than sixteen years before had started his own company to design and manufacture cot systems for air ambulances. We thoroughly enjoyed meeting Ralph and his wife and sharing with them the mission of Grace on Wings. They wished us well in our new ministry and promised to look for us at the AMTC conference the following year.

By 2009, we were beginning to feel God prompt us to take the next step, which was to become an ALS provider. Once again we would have to purchase expensive medical equipment, recruit more highly trained volunteer medical personnel, and go before the Indiana State EMS Commission to answer God's call. But the Grace on Wings Board of Directors had no doubt that God was leading us forward and would help us climb that next mountain.

Though we were doing great work as a start-up ministry, the need to take the next step, to become a fully credentialed ALS air ambulance, weighed heavily on my mind. How would God provide?

Dinner Gala

The first annual Grace on Wings Dinner Gala was held on the University of Indianapolis campus in February of 2009. This event, much like the annual fall hog roast event we'd been having, was established primarily to increase awareness of our ministry and also to give thanks for the blessings we had received throughout the year. Although we hoped to gain new supporters, the purpose of the gala was not primarily to raise funds.

Our guest speaker was Donna Thomas, the woman whose counsel we had sought as Grace on Wings was being conceived. The main theme Donna stressed during her talk was to live a life that cried out, "Why not!" instead of "I can't." She shared some of the salient features of her mission endeavors spanning nearly sixty years. Donna challenged everyone present to start each day by saying, "Lord, who do want me to reach out to today?" Ben and Betsy James, Pastor Gary Walker's daughter and her husband, provided the evening's music.

Hal had thought it would be appropriate to recognize individuals or corporations that had had a major impact on the success of our ministry. He had found someone who could make an exact replica of Nellie in model form. His idea was that the "Nellie Award" would be presented annually at the gala to a worthy recipient or recipients.

That evening the first Nellie Award went to George Schulp, the president of the Superior Ambulance Service. George was so taken by the mission of Grace on Wings that he'd donated all of the ground ambulance service to our patients whenever his crews were available to transfer our patients to and from Nellie. Often the cost of a ground ambulance from the hospital to the plane, or vice versa, would be $700 to $800, even for a distance of a few miles. So the charitable contribution by Superior Ambulance was not inconsequential.

We were thankful for all of the people who attended that first gala and for the contributions to the ministry so many individuals had made. Yet I felt some disappointment more people had not responded to the call to become a part of what God was doing through Grace on Wings.

I was reminded of the parable Jesus told about the great banquet in the gospel of Luke (Luke 14:15–24). In this parable, the great banquet is the kingdom of God. Jesus essentially tells us the blessings of the kingdom are available to all who come to Christ by faith. And yet the story points out all of the excuses the people gave for not attending the feast.

I pondered the parallels and what God was teaching me about the need for each of us to examine ourselves openly and honestly before God. To what extent are we like those who have little or no time for God or the work he calls us to? Do we fully realize our sinful nature and our need for a loving, forgiving relationship with God, one that will compel us to join him in the sacred work he is doing to reach out to those who need him and to serve the poor and needy among us? The invitation to the great banquet has been sent, and the table is prepared. Who will come and join in his gala?

Connor's Story

Connor M., an 18-year-old young man from Indianapolis, went to Breckenridge, Colorado, on a ski trip with his father and brother. The trip had been planned for nearly a year, but his life would be changed in an instant. Connor sustained a broken femur in a snow-boarding accident on the Breckenridge slopes. He was hospitalized for surgical repair of the broken leg. On the third day after surgery, he was released to recuperate in a hotel room. Connor still required some oxygen by nasal cannula (a lightweight tube delivering supplemental oxygen through two prongs placed in the nostrils).

That night Connor's brother heard him snoring loudly. The next morning his brother and father could not wake him. He was taken to the Emergency Room, where it was confirmed he had suffered brain injury from insufficient oxygen. He was in a coma. That's when Grace on Wings answered a call for help.

Tami wrote the Mission Report for this patient, recording the following details.

His mom flew out to be with him, and his parents were told he'd probably be in a vegetative state permanently. Connor's mom contacted his sister attending college in Michigan. She enlisted the Campus Crusade for Christ group for prayer while Connor's parents called for prayers from their church in Indianapolis. Soon over a thousand people were praying for Connor's recovery. Two days later, Connor opened his eyes.

Connor told his mother, "I died and was on the ladder going up to heaven when I was made to turn around because so many people were praying for me."

The flight from Denver to Indianapolis was uneventful, and Connor was taken to the Rehab Institute of Indiana for further treatment. Two weeks into recovery, Connor was reading thousands of Facebook communications from all of his prayer warriors. He wrote, "I should have been dead. I was on a set of stairs, an escalator of sorts, but instead of going up as I would to approach heaven, I was on my way back down."

When asked if it was the many prayers pulling him back, he said, "I was overwhelmed by how much I was loved. I know this was a miracle from God. It wasn't chance, luck, or a medical procedure, but a miracle."

"We were amazed by his miracle story and were so glad to be a part of getting him home," Tami wrote.

One year after his life-altering accident, Connor attended the Grace on Wings Gala event with his parents. It was there we learned that the stroke had damaged the language area of the brain, causing him to have difficulty finding the right words to communicate at times, yet he was finishing high school and making plans to attend Ivy Tech to learn a trade.

Connor had no trouble finding the right words that night to describe his relationship with the Lord. "I know everything happens for a reason. Before the accident, I was not very adaptable to change. I knew Jesus Christ as my Savior, but I was not very committed in showing my faith. Today I am empowered and so very grateful God spared me to enjoy this wonderful life. I am so satisfied and comfortable in my life and at peace with whatever comes. It is such a God thing."

As Jesus' brother James said, "The prayer of a righteous man is powerful and effective" (James 5:16).

The Power Of Prayer

Knowing and serving God better means leaning into prayer more and more. Connor's story is evidence. So, too, is the story of Amy Crawford, one of our volunteers.

Once when I was in college, I had occasion to drive by myself through Indianapolis. Just as I entered the downtown area on I-65 South, a helicopter lifted off the top of Methodist Hospital on its way to pick up a patient. I was distracted by the sight of the helicopter but knew what it was and what type of missions it flew. I have always recalled what happened next as one of the moments God has used in my life to show His power!

I had prayed many times in my life previous to that time. It's what Christians "do," right? So I prayed then, right at that moment, that God would save the person who was to be airlifted. Immediately I felt a sense of peace come over me and a surety that the patient would be okay! I never heard who the person was or the outcome of the trauma faced, but for the first time ever, I experienced that "peace that passes understanding." I have never forgotten it.

Many years later, I am often blessed by that same inexplicable sense of "peace" when I receive the prayer requests and notifications that Grace on Wings is flying to pick up a patient. It is a joy and a privilege to be a part of the praying group for this wonderful ministry. I know I can't pilot a plane. I can't take care of a patient in need of health care. I can't drive an ambulance. But I can pray for safety of the flight crew and patient, and I can lift the patient before God to be healed.

I often pray for the message of the gospel to sink deeply into the hearts of the patient and his/her family members so their journey to their earthly home can just be a layover on their way to their eternal home in heaven with Jesus. I know God hears those prayers, and I am always grateful for the post-flight reports that the volunteers write. The testimonies speak deeply of the peace that the gospel of Jesus brings into our lives during times of crises. Grace on Wings continues to "wow my heart" as it is used to show Christ to those in need!

10

Following His Lead
("Here, There, And Everywhere")

In between patient flights, much of our time during the spring of 2009 was spent making the necessary preparations for raising the level of medical care from basic life support (BLS) to advanced life support (ALS). It was a step we wanted to make to better meet our mission and serve those contacting us for assistance.

The first thing we had to do was find a hospital that would agree to be our "supervising hospital." According to the guidelines established by the Indiana State Emergency Medical Services (EMS) Commission, all ALS providers must have such an arrangement, whether they are providing services on the ground or in the air.

Because of my longstanding affiliation with the St. Vincent Frankfort Hospital, I approached Tom Crawford, CEO of the hospital, to see if he would be willing to undertake such a venture. Tom is a good Christian man who is always willing to serve others in our community. He was aware of the Grace on Wings ministry and was happy to assist us in advancing to ALS care. St. Vincent Frankfort Hospital became our official supporting hospital.

Next, Eric Frantz, our chief paramedic and invaluable to our early success, worked with Tami and me to write the new ALS medical protocols. These protocols established guidelines for the treatment of any medical situation our staff might encounter. Since the medical crews volunteering for Grace on Wings would come from many different hospital and paramedic services, it was imperative to standardize the care of our patients. Eric also collaborated with Tami to procure the required additional equipment and put together medic bags for our flights.

Tami was able to get an arrangement with Hendricks Community Hospital to obtain controlled substances we would need to treat our patients in flight. In addition, the North Central Health Service Foundation gave us a grant for $20,000 to purchase a refurbished monitor/defibrillator.

Things were coming together nicely for the change in our service. Most of the time the ministry team and its board members were extremely humbled that God had allowed us to be a part of the ministry he had given us. But occasionally misplaced ambition would raise its ugly head and seek to lead us astray. One such occasion occurred in late spring of 2009.

Clarifying Our Call

A friend of our ministry came to us with the idea of starting a "Grace on Wings West" base in Kansas where he lived. He visited with our board and shared his vision for expanding our ministry by establishing a branch office there with volunteer pilots and medical crews. He said he hoped to provide the same ministry to patients we were by using the same vision and mission statements.

The idea at first made a lot of sense, as we had received numerous requests from patients in the western U.S. we could not serve because the distance and cost were prohibitive. By opening a second base of operations, we could certainly reach more patients and share the love of Christ with them. We were also flying a significant portion of our missions to and from Florida. Maybe we should also start a "Grace on Wings South" in Florida while we were at it!

Hal made a trip to Kansas and met with a small group of friends there in order to see if a second base of operations was feasible. Although the idea had merit, Hal soon realized the infrastructure was not in place to start a new base of operations. The timing was not right.

Fortunately, before we could go any further, Pastor Gary reminded us God was the one leading our ministry, and we should not get out ahead of him. The realization hit us hard, and we halted our plans. We almost took off running when we had just learned to crawl.

Worthy Of Praise

In July of 2009, Hal again went before the Indiana State EMS Commission and asked that the waiver we had been operating under be removed. Since all air ambulances were classified as an ALS service, it had been necessary for Grace on Wings to receive a waiver allowing us to operate under a BLS certification until that time. It was the final step needed for Grace on Wings to become a fully accredited ALS air ambulance provider. There was unanimous agreement by the Commission, and we again received their praise for the work of the ministry.

Later that year, we received another affirmation of our calling. The Oshkosh Air Show, the biggest and most prestigious gathering of aviation enthusiasts in the world, invited Grace on Wings to set up a display. The show's theme for 2009 was "Fly4Life," and it would feature many missionary organizations.

Nellie was prominently located very near one of the main attractions, the Airbus A380. That location offered us a lot of traffic and attention. It was quite a thrill and an honor to share the story of Grace on Wings with people who were so passionate about aviation. But even more importantly, we passed out Bibles and shared the gospel with everyone we could.

God continued to show us favor that year. We had been offered a larger office/hangar space in the Hawker-Beechcraft building on the general aviation side of the Indianapolis International Airport. When we moved our office to gain the much-needed space, we discovered we had access to a nicely furnished waiting area. Most of the time this area sat vacant. The room was nearly twice the size of our office and contained several meeting tables and comfortable chairs. A kitchen containing a refrigerator and microwave oven sat adjacent to the spacious waiting area. We wondered what God had in mind for this space, and we soon found out.

At the time we were flying an average of one to two days per week, so we had plenty of down time in the office waiting for flight requests and dealing with day-to-day operations. One day I said to Hal, "Maybe we could start a Bible study in the empty waiting area." He liked the idea and thought we should invite some workers from the neighboring Hawker-Beechcraft maintenance complex to join us.

On September 2, 2009, we held the first of what would become our weekly Bible study. Five people were in attendance. Paul Powell, David Voorhies, and Myron Wilson joined Hal and me as we began a study of the book of John. The number of people attending varied occasionally, but the initial group remained quite small.

In the beginning, we all brought a sack lunch, as time for the study was limited. One week Becky, my wife, volunteered to make lunch for the people at the Bible study, and it was very well received. She offered to continue making home-cooked meals, and the number of people attending steadily grew. Three years later, we had a steady gathering of twenty to twenty-five each Wednesday to study God's Word and pray together.

Many of these dear brothers and sisters have volunteered in various ways for our ministry. Through this rich experience, we have come to realize how important it is to be immersed continually in the word of God so that we are adequately prepared to share the love of Christ whenever the opportunity should arise.

For The Cross

In the fall of 2009, a missionary friend contacted me. He and I had served on a mission team together in the mountains of northern Pakistan following a devastating earthquake in 2005, which killed approximately 700,000 people and left more than 3,000,000 people homeless. He said he was leading a mission team to the West Bank and Gaza regions of Israel to work with Palestinian Christians and learn more about their plight.

He asked me to join him, and I said yes. I would be able to work alongside a doctor in a local clinic just outside Bethlehem. By this time, I had been involved in mission trips to Turkey, the Kurdish region of northern Iraq, and Pakistan. I was eager to be a part of this journey as well to experience life on both sides of the Israeli/ Palestinian conflict.

While in Beit Sahour, the predominantly Christian suburb of Bethlehem, I had the pleasure of meeting Dr. Johnny, a local physician working in an outpatient clinic there. Dr. Johnny introduced me to many wonderful people and gave me a glimpse of the everyday struggles of the Palestinian people. Although many of his family had left Palestine to escape persecution at the hands of both Muslims and Jews, Dr. Johnny was committed to staying in his homeland and continuing to minister to his patients.

One day Ibtisam, a nurse working with Dr. Johnny at the clinic, took me to the Greek Orthodox Christian school nearby to meet her husband, Emil. He was the headmaster at the school. Emil gave me a tour of the school and the city of Beit Sahour. On the tour, he told me the average unemployment rate in the Bethlehem region was 50 to 60 percent.

"After the second Intifada (uprising)," Emil said, "the Israeli army erected a thirty-foot high cement wall around our city, isolating us from the places where most of our people worked. Now the Palestinian people must do whatever they can to survive."

He then took me to a small neighborhood workshop in Beit Sahour where I witnessed several craftsmen skillfully making crosses, nativity scenes, and other beautiful creations from one of the most plentiful items to be found in Palestine, olive wood. As I stood there holding a newly made olive wood cross, God revealed to me a way to help these Palestinian workers while simultaneously providing Grace on Wings patients with a tangible reminder of their flight with us.

"Emil, can these workers make one hundred olive wood crosses with "Grace on Wings" carved into the wood and ship them to me in the United States?" I asked.

"Of course, no problem. You want more, we make more," he said.

Since then, every Grace on Wings patient has received an olive wood cross made in Bethlehem. The cross is given to them, along with a Bible, at the beginning of their flight. It is a joy to see the patients take comfort, grasping their crosses during the flight, holding tightly to them as one would cling to a life preserver while being tossed to and fro during a violent storm at sea.

God has continued to use Palestinian Christians living in the birthplace of Jesus to bless the patients we serve nearly half a world away! Many of these Christians, like Dr. Johnny, choose to remain in Palestine, where they comprise perhaps just 5 percent of the population. Each day they struggle to make a living so they can support their families. And yet God has found a way for us to work together with them for his glory.

11

All Things Through Christ
("Heart Of A Lion")

A variety of challenges were maturing the ministry and everyone associated with it. We were becoming more adept at managing the transport of patients with complex medical problems as we gained valuable experience through the performance of many more missions. We saw God at work in the ministry, but sometimes it was difficult to see him at work in the lives of our patients. He was there all along, however, transforming broken lives in ways we could never imagine.

One day in June of 2010, Tami called me and said, "Dr. Jim, we have an urgent flight request to transfer a young woman from Washington, D.C., to Chicago. You won't believe what happened to her!"

Tami proceeded to disclose the tragic details of the case involving Amy Wooddell, a previously vibrant, 24-year-old professional dance instructor who found herself literally fighting for her life. Tami's call set in motion my role as Medical Director to oversee the medical aspects of Amy's Grace on Wings flight. At the time of her flight, all I knew of Amy was the medical information in her chart. But over the next three years, I would learn so much more about Amy's life from discussions with her and her family.

Amy's Story, Part 1

The beginning of 2010 was magical for Amy Wooddell. Shortly after graduating from Texas Christian University with a degree in modern dance, wedding bells rang for her and her longtime boyfriend, Jonny. After the wedding, the two of them settled into married life in their home in suburban Overland Park, Kansas. Just four months later, her life would change dramatically and forever.

Amy grew up in Shawnee, Kansas, a western suburb of Kansas City, as the second child born to her parents, Sue and Bruce Gardner. Her passion for dance began at age five and continued to evolve through her school years to include lessons in ballet, tap, lyrical, and jazz. In addition to dance, she began tumbling classes in the second grade and routinely won top honors during competitive contests.

As a teenager, Amy was involved in cheerleading and the school band and chorus group. These activities were in addition to her six dance classes per week. By age fourteen, she was teaching dance to younger students while continuing to advance her own skills. Although she was quiet and reserved by nature, Amy was a self-starter and a very determined individual, whether in school or in extracurricular activities. Little did she know the self-discipline, patience, and perseverance she learned as a dancer would serve her so well during the life-threatening crisis that would one day strike her down.

Amy attended the local Methodist church with her family and believed in God. She was very active in the church youth group. After church camp following her freshman year in high school, she had a renewed enthusiasm for worshiping God, something very noticeable to her parents. A few years later, she went through confirmation class and openly professed her faith in Jesus Christ as her Lord and Savior.

Following high school graduation, Amy attended a local college, where she met her future husband, Jonny Wooddell. Although the two had attended the same high school in Shawnee, they had never dated, as they had different interests and different sets of friends. Amy caught Jonny's attention during an ethics class one day, and he was smitten immediately. He unashamedly made his friend change seats with him so that he could sit beside Amy from then on.

Amy and Jonny dated for almost a year before he inexplicably broke up with her and transferred to Kansas State University. She then transferred to Texas Christian University, where she immersed herself in her college coursework and grueling dance instruction. It would be eighteen months until their lives intersected again. Jonny would later confess that breaking up with Amy was the biggest mistake of his life.

Jonny had a strong faith in God due to his sound religious upbringing at the First Baptist Church in Shawnee. He attended church twice on Sundays and again every Wednesday evening. He could not have imagined then how important his upbringing would be, how much he would come to rely on God to help him through the darkest days of his life many years in the future.

Although his life appeared normal on the surface, Jonny was no stranger to adversity. At age seven, he was diagnosed with the rare condition of renal artery stenosis, a decrease in the diameter of the blood vessels carrying blood from the heart to the kidneys. Renal artery stenosis causes reduced blood flow to the kidneys and an abnormally high blood pressure. Before the diagnosis, his blood pressure was measured at a dangerously high level of 250/149. Normal for his age should have been around 85/40.

Jonny's parents took him to see a renowned vascular surgeon at the University of Michigan. Jonny subsequently underwent a total of five serious vascular surgeries over the next few years, culminating in the surgical removal of one of his kidneys when he was in the seventh grade.

Through his childhood medical problems, Jonny came to understand and accept that he often had no control over his circumstances. But he believed God was in control and had put him where he was to prepare him for something later on in life. During long periods of confinement in the hospital, he would study the Bible to find strength and comfort. His favorite verse was Joshua 1:9, "Have I not commanded you? Be strong and courageous. Do not be terrified; do not be discouraged, for the LORD your God will be with you wherever you go."

Amy and Jonny reconnected nearly eighteen months after their breakup. At the time she was thoroughly engrossed in her college studies, attending classes from 8 a.m. until 4 p.m., Monday through Friday, at TCU. She then would take a short break for an hour and a half for dinner before participating in dance rehearsal for three hours.

Jonny put a lot of miles on his truck driving from Manhattan, Kansas, to Fort Worth, Texas, twice a month while trying to win Amy back. Many times she was too busy to hang out with him, but their relationship was rekindled. A year later, during Amy's last semester in school, Jonny and Amy were engaged to be married.

Amy had made plans to teach dance and choreograph her own pieces in the Kansas City area after graduation. She was even considering starting her own dance company. Life was full of promise at that moment in time, and Amy and Jonny were feeling on top of the world.

Four months after their wedding, Amy made plans to fly to Washington, D.C., with her mother and father to attend the law school graduation of her older brother, Brad, while Jonny would be staying at home to continue working.

The Unexpected Crisis

The day before Amy was to leave, she experienced nagging shoulder pain, a condition for which she had sought treatment from a local chiropractor in the past. She went to the chiropractor at 5 p.m. that day. The following day, she departed for D.C. by plane in the company of her parents, as scheduled.

Upon arriving, Amy was very busy sightseeing, shopping, and preparing for the graduation ceremonies. By late afternoon, she began to feel ill from being dizzy. Then she became nauseated and noted some blurriness to her vision. She told her mother she was too sick to attend the dinner reception with her family that evening. Instead, she would to stay in the hotel room to rest.

The next morning, Amy felt terrible. She couldn't walk straight, couldn't stop vomiting, was light-headed, and complained of severe neck pain. Amy's mother took her to a nearby hospital emergency room. After a 13-hour marathon evaluation, she was diagnosed with vertigo, given medication, and released.

Her mother, Sue, was given several prescriptions to get filled for Amy. By that time of night, no nearby pharmacies were open, so she took Amy back to the hotel in hopes that her condition would improve with rest and the passage of time.

That night Amy awoke from sleep when her legs began to tremble uncontrollably and she felt hot all over her body. Knowing she was in trouble, she aroused her mother from sleep. Her mom thought a cool bath might make her feel better. The bath provided no relief, and Amy's condition continued to worsen.

Standing up shakily, Amy said, "Mom, there's something really wrong with me. You need to take me to the hospital."

Sue had her lie down on the floor, and then Amy passed out. She slurred her words and mumbled incoherently as her mother cried out, "Stay with me, Amy! Stay with me!" Amy's father called 911, and Sue kept calling out, "Amy, stay with me!"

Suddenly Amy opened her eyes and spoke very clearly, "Jesus saved me." Then she lapsed into unconsciousness.

Amy was rushed by ambulance to the hospital, where she was diagnosed with a dissected vertebral artery that led to a severe brain stem stroke from a blood clot in the basilar artery. She underwent a 7.5-hour emergency procedure. A potent blood thinner, TPA, was administered to break up the clot causing her stroke. An interventional radiologist then placed stents in the torn right vertebral artery.

Jonny, still at home in Kansas City, was notified of Amy's stroke. He immediately called his father, David Wooddell, who said he would drop everything and travel to D.C. with him right away. He had just enough airline points to purchase two one-way tickets.

When Jonny and David arrived at Amy's bedside following her lengthy initial procedure, Amy seemed alert and talkative and in no distress. They left the hospital that night thinking the worst was passed. After checking into a hotel, however, they were notified by the hospital that Amy had just suffered a massive intracranial bleed. The doctors concluded she would need an immediate craniotomy to relieve the pressure on her brain. Even then, the neurosurgeon said, she might not survive through the night. At that moment, hope nearly vanished.

Later that same night, Amy underwent extensive neurosurgery, including a decompressive craniectomy (removal of part of the skull to relieve pressure on the brain). Following the surgery, the neurosurgeon advised Jonny and the family that 85 percent of patients in Amy's condition did not survive.

To make matters worse, a few days after surgery, Amy was afflicted with bacterial meningitis, a life-threatening infection of the brain and its covering layer. It occurred as a consequence of having tubes placed in the brain to keep the swelling down.

Amy was in a coma for several days. When she awoke, she was completely paralyzed and unable to speak. Her doctors were concerned she had fallen into the "locked-in" syndrome, a condition in which she may be aware and awake but cannot move or communicate verbally due to complete paralysis of nearly all voluntary muscles in the body except for the eyes. The doctors told the family, "Even if she survives, she will probably never speak or walk again."

During this time, Amy could see those who came to visit, but she couldn't talk or move. She tried to communicate by blinking her eyes but became frustrated when she couldn't make her desires known. Jonny and David carried out a bedside vigil, with Jonny staying with Amy as long as the hospital would allow. They prayed for God to perform a miracle by healing Amy. David focused his prayers on 1 Samuel 14:6, "Perhaps the LORD will act in our behalf." They knew their only hope was with God, not man.

Jonny and Rachel, a dear friend of Amy's, explained to Amy exactly what had happened to her. He said those in charge of her care were going to work hard, and she would get better day by day. He knew from his own medical crises that the doctors and nurses could do only so much. He put all of his trust in God to provide a miracle of healing for his new bride. Although there was little hope for recovery being expressed by her caregivers, Jonny knew all things were possible with God.

Jonny's friends provided much needed support and encouragement. Some came to visit in Washington while others took care of the house back in Kansas. One friend even repainted the bathroom the color Amy had chosen from her ICU bed by communicating her choice to them by blinking her eyes. Jeremy, a good friend of Jonny, told him, "Amy has the heart of a lion."

The hospital nurses were surprised Jonny was still constantly by Amy's side. They told him the husband usually leaves and allows the family to take over in a situation like theirs. Those thoughts were completely foreign to Jonny and served only to make him more steadfastly determined to love his wife as God intended, according to the sacred vows he had spoken a few short months before. In support of his decision, many of Jonny's coworkers at Sprint gave up their paid time off and cancelled vacations to cover Jonny during his three-month absence so he could be by Amy's side.

When it became apparent that Amy's hospital stay would be protracted and indefinite, God provided for Amy's family through the loving gifts of many friends and acquaintances. Mary and Ken, friends and Navigator associates, offered Jonny and David the use of a house in Arlington, Virginia, for their month-long ordeal. The Navigator prayer network was also utilized, and Amy then had the prayers of saints everywhere going up to God on her behalf.

Jonny's father, David, began journaling the events of each day and posting online the insights and Scriptures the Holy Spirit led him to in dealing with this crisis. "Pop's Journals," as Jonny affectionately called them, impacted the lives of people all over the world who learned of Amy's plight through this forum. Prayers and words of support and encouragement poured in, and they were like a breath of fresh air to the family just when they were most needed.

For Jonny's mother, Dinah, the nightmare scenario took on a totally different form. When her husband left Kansas City to be by Jonny's side, Dinah remained at home alone nearly a thousand miles away. She suffered in silence but served as a mighty prayer warrior, constantly interceding for Amy and her family before the Lord.

Earlier that spring, Dinah had planted one of her favorite trees, a crape myrtle, outside her home. As was typical of the tree, it looked like a bare stick, incapable of bringing forth any life, when it was first planted in the ground. Dinah patiently watched for the tree to show signs of life each day during the endless, lonely moments at home.

One day Jonny and his father met with some of Amy's doctors in a small room just outside of the ICU. The doctors said Amy would most likely never be able to move again. At that moment, Amy's friend, Rachel, came into the room sobbing. "Amy moved her pinky!" she exclaimed. Everyone hurried into the ICU room to find Amy surrounded by four nurses, all wiping tears from their cheeks. God had given them a miracle. Amy had moved!

Jonny excitedly called his mother in Kansas City to inform her of the renewed hope he felt. His mother said she knew recovery was still a long way off, but she believed God was indeed providing an answer to their prayers.

After speaking with Jonny, Dinah went outside to tend to her plants. To her amazement, her previously dormant crape myrtle tree had exploded with bright pink blossoms! She was convinced God had breathed new life into Amy and she would continue to blossom just as her precious crape myrtle had.

Next Up: Grace On Wings

Although Amy remained extremely weak and susceptible to setbacks from infection or recurrent bleeding, each day she slowly improved. After a month in the intensive care unit, Amy's condition finally had improved enough to allow her to be transferred to a rehabilitation center to begin the long process of recovery.

Jonny and the family were then faced with several major decisions they had not considered until that moment. Where should they take Amy for her rehabilitation to maximize her recovery? And, equally as important, how would they get her to the rehab facility safely once she was accepted?

Jonny first set about trying to find the best rehab institute available and then to see whether Amy would be a candidate for admission. He performed an extensive online search and discovered The Rehabilitation Institute of Chicago (RIC), widely recognized as the premier rehab hospital in America for over twenty years. When he contacted RIC, he was greatly relieved to hear that treatment of patients recovering from a stroke, even one as devastating as Amy's, was one of their areas of expertise.

After much paperwork and the help of the case manager at the hospital, Amy was accepted at RIC. Then Jonny wondered, "How are we going to transfer Amy from downtown Washington, D.C., to Chicago?"

He first considered a ground ambulance transport but quickly realized Amy's condition was much too fragile to tolerate a long and arduous ride clear across the country. He also learned such a transport would have been prohibitively expensive. Amy, her doctors told Jonny, must be quickly transferred by an air ambulance fully equipped to care for critically ill patients.

Jonny again searched the Internet, this time for air ambulances. He found several air ambulance companies and contacted each one to receive a quote. He was shocked and disheartened to discover the cost of transferring Amy would be nearly $30,000, and the insurance company would not cover the expense.

Jonny sought guidance from his family and asked his church for prayer support. Amy's mother told Jonny she had heard about a Christian organization called Grace on Wings that had recently transported a relative of one of her friends. Jonny contacted Grace on Wings immediately and talked with Hal. He was once again filled with hope when Hal told him Grace on Wings could transport Amy for just $7,400, the cost to the ministry for fuel, maintenance, and ground transportation. Jonny told Hal he would find a way to get the money.

Some donations were coming in, but a large deficit of $6,700 still remained. That night as Jonny was eating dinner with his father and his brother-in-law, Brad, a phone text message notification interrupted their conversation. Jonny glanced at his phone and said, "Huh, somebody just donated $67 on Paypal for Amy's transfer."

Jonny's dad thought it sounded like an odd amount and asked, "Are you sure it says $67?"

Jonny examined the text message more closely and said, "I don't believe it. Someone donated the whole $6,700, not $67!" The text message indicated the money had been sent already to Grace on Wings.

Jonny found out the amount was sent by a young couple from his church, Joe and DeAnna, who had heard about Amy's stroke and the urgent need for funds to get Amy to Chicago. When he contacted

Joe to thank him, Joe said simply, "It was God's money, we had it, and Amy needed it. We were just glad to help."

God Makes A Way

Tami communicated with Jonny for several days to make the necessary preparations for the flight. Jonny explained the importance of having Amy discharged from the hospital by 11 a.m. on June 22, 2010, as her insurance required. Also, he stressed how fragile Amy's condition was and his concern that a long ground ambulance ride from the hospital to the plane might cause her more harm.

For those reasons, Tami pleaded with Hal to try to obtain permission for the Grace on Wings plane to land at the Ronald Reagan Airport, located just five miles from the hospital in downtown D.C., instead of Dulles International Airport, a 45-minute drive from the hospital. No way, thought Hal. He knew no small aircraft had been given permission to fly in or out of Reagan Airport since the devastating terrorist attacks on our nation on September 11, 2001. Nonetheless, he contacted the Transportation Safety Authority (TSA) and requested authorization to land at Reagan Airport as an air ambulance making an emergency medical evacuation.

The TSA personnel were not optimistic about the chances for such an approval. They told Hal to submit the appropriate paperwork and see what happened. Hal painstakingly completed the voluminous federal documents, attached a letter of medical necessity from the hospital, and forwarded the entire package to the TSA as required.

A week passed by without any response from the TSA. Hal had all but given up on the idea of flying to Reagan Airport. Reluctantly, Hal and Tami made plans to fly the mission using Dulles Airport, despite the inherent difficulties this would bring.

Jonny and his family had seen God at work in saving Amy's life. She had miraculously survived a stroke when it looked as though she would be unable to speak or move ever again. Potential setbacks loomed like storm clouds on the horizon. Amy would need God to intervene in a mighty way once again to speed her recovery.

The morning of June 22, 2010, heavy thunderstorms blanketed the Indianapolis area, causing a delay in the crew's planned departure time. While waiting for the weather to clear, Tami talked by cell phone with Amy's husband, Jonny. She explained the situation and apologized for the delay.

At the same time, from the far corner of the office, Hal heard the fax machine proclaim the arrival of an incoming message. Retrieving the fax, Hal quickly scanned the pages and shouted to Tami, "I don't believe it! The TSA gave us their approval to use Reagan Airport. Praise God!"

Suddenly the tears in Tami's eyes, which moments before were born of disappointment, became tears of joy at the recognition of how God had just performed a miracle before their very eyes.

12

Parting The Seas
("Houston, We Have A Problem")

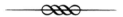

Grace on Wings' involvement in the lives of its patients goes far beyond the mechanics of transport. God uses Grace on Wings to transform broken lives and help traumatized people heal spiritually as well as physically. By sharing the love of Christ, we develop lifelong relationships with the patients and families we serve. Most importantly, through it all, God is glorified.

Amy's Story, Part 2

With the TSA waiver authorization in hand, the crew hastily departed Indianapolis to take advantage of the improving weather conditions. Like Tami, they were elated to be in the air and part of what would be a life-changing mission for Amy and ultimately many others in the future. They were humbled, as well, by how God was making a way where there seemed to be none. Climbing to altitude, Hal said, "God parted the storms for us just like he parted the Red Sea for the Israelites fleeing Egypt."

Although the flight to Washington, D.C., was quick and uneventful, Hal still had a vague, uneasy feeling gnawing at the back of his mind as Washington Center flight control handed him off to Potomac Approach Control.

Having flown out of the D.C. area hundreds of times with Eastern Airlines and freight carriers nearly twenty years before, Hal knew the traffic pattern well. As the crew passed over Dulles Airport at 7,000 feet, the Potomac Approach controller began vectoring the plane in a holding pattern with a series of turns. Hal immediately knew something was wrong.

"Medevac 910 November Foxtrot, did you activate the TSA waiver?" the controller asked.

"Roger, Potomac. I have the authorization here in my hand with the confirmation number," Hal responded confidently.

After a momentary silence, the Potomac controller replied. "Roger, Medevac 910 November Foxtrot, you are cleared to the restricted area. When you get on the ground, I need you to call this number."

Hal wrote down the number he was given. He knew that anytime a pilot was asked to call someone after landing, it was an ominous sign.

"What did I do wrong?" he asked hesitantly.

The controller's reply was curt. "The man standing behind me just says to call the number when you get on the ground."

Hal had to put aside his concerns quickly and regain his focus, as he was being vectored to the approach to Reagan Airport located on the west bank of the Potomac River. So much had changed since he had last flown this approach. Since the terrorist attacks of 9/11/2001, in the interest of national security, no general aviation flights had been allowed to land at Reagan Airport.

As the plane descended rapidly over the Arlington National Cemetery, Hal and the crew peered out the windows on the left side of the plane and could see the Lincoln Memorial in the foreground with the reflecting pool pointing the way eastward to the Washington Monument towering over the landscape. The approach took the plane directly over the Pentagon at an altitude of only 200 feet just seconds before the wheels screeched with the reassuring sound of contact with the runway.

Hal expeditiously taxied off of the active runway, searching for the expected "Follow Me" truck to lead him to a parking space; however, none came to meet the aircraft. Suddenly Hal saw a TSA agent barreling out of the terminal with arms crossed above his head in an X pattern, signifying the plane needed to stop immediately. Hal brought the plane to a sudden halt, shut down the engines, and then opened the aft compartment door to the outside. In his hand, he clutched the TSA waiver granting the crew permission to land at the airport and the phone number he was instructed to call after landing.

As he jumped onto the tarmac, Hal saw two military gunships landing on either side of his plane. The TSA agent shouted gruffly, "Who the hell are you people, and who gave you permission to land here?"

Handing the agent the paperwork authorizing the flight, Hal explained that the crew had been given a waiver by the TSA to land at the airport to facilitate the medical evacuation of a patient hospitalized at a medical center nearby. Furthermore, Hal told the agent, he was supposed to contact the TSA by phone immediately. He showed the agent the telephone number the Potomac Approach controller had given him.

The agent led Hal into his office and allowed him to make the call. Hal discovered the TSA official who had originally authorized the flight had failed to properly activate the waiver. A great deal of confusion and alarm occurred until the situation could be sorted out. To his great relief, eventually Hal was assured he had indeed conducted himself appropriately and according to TSA protocol.

"Heart Of A Lion" Video

The Grace on Wings medical team was whisked away by a local ambulance crew to the hospital to prepare the patient for the transport to the Rehab Institute of Chicago as planned. Meanwhile, Hal was busy activating the remainder of the flight plan and checking the weather between D.C. and Chicago.

Once at the hospital, the medical team evaluated Amy and got her ready to take to the plane for the transfer. Jonny was there and was making a video of the whole transfer process, which he later posted on YouTube with the title "Heart of a Lion."

As the medical team arrived at the aircraft with Amy, the TSA agent who had initially reprimanded Hal asked him about the mission of Grace on Wings and the significance of the prominent red cross on the tail of our aircraft. Hal took the opportunity to share the gospel message with him and explained why we do what we do—show the love of Christ through aviation—because Jesus showed his love for us by sacrificing himself on the cross for our sins.

Just before loading Amy onto the aircraft prior to departure, Hal led the team in prayer over her. The TSA agent was so moved by what he witnessed and learned about the ministry of Grace on Wings he subsequently became one of our faithful monthly supporters!

With nearly a dozen commercial airlines operating out of Reagan Airport, the line of jets awaiting clearance for takeoff was impressive. As an air ambulance performing a medical evacuation of a critical patient, however, Hal received first priority for takeoff. He taxied around the massive commercial airliners to the hold line on the active runway. From there he could see the quizzical look on the faces of the passengers aboard the jets.

At that moment, Hal and the crew were humbled by their role in this unfolding story. The eyes of those passengers focused on the beautiful red cross on the aircraft's tail as it went by. What an honor it was to bring glory to the Lord by serving in that small way!

Chicago's Challenges

At The Rehabilitation Institute of Chicago, Amy received extensive sessions of grueling physical therapy, occupational therapy, and speech therapy for nearly a month. Many times she was pushed to tears as she would fight through the pain, nausea, and frustration during the arduous recovery. In the midst of her pain, she would keep reciting Philippians 4:13, "I can do everything through him who gives me strength."

Amy's main physical therapist was a woman named Preeti, whose job it was to push Amy hard during therapy so she would have maximum recovery. One day Amy's goal during therapy was to stand for thirty seconds, which required a superhuman effort for someone like Amy who had been bedridden for over a month. After ten seconds, Amy began to cry in pain from the tremendous strain on her weakened body. She pleaded with Preeti to take her back to bed, but Preeti said, "I don't ever want to hear you say you want to go back to bed. What do you want to do, stay in bed the rest of your life? Use your energy to get well, not to tell me you want to go back to bed."

Amy was so angry, she told me later. She cried and cried, but she did not go back to bed. Only as she began to gain strength and walk again did she come to appreciate the loving and challenging care she had received from Preeti.

One thing Amy said she craved throughout her recovery was popsicles. Until she could pass a "swallow test," she was told, popsicles were off limits. When she did pass the test, a rehab caseworker went out and bought her a box of orange popsicles. It was her first solid food since the stroke, and she ate nearly the whole box by herself. With her lips stained orange, she said, "I love popsicles. I love Jonny!"

Ken and Mary, Jonny's father's friends from The Navigators ministry who had helped with the emergency housing needs in Washington, visited Amy several times while she was hospitalized. They heard Amy tell Jonny she wanted to go to Hawaii when she got better. Mary said, "I will get you to Hawaii." So they made all of the necessary arrangements to send Amy and Jonny to Hawaii and provide for their housing while they were there.

Amy and Jonny did enjoy an all-expenses-paid, one-week vacation in Hawaii after leaving the center in Chicago, just three months after the beginning of Amy's life-threatening crisis. Although she was still plagued with frequent bouts of dizziness, nausea, vomiting, and limited mobility, the tropical respite was like heaven to the beleaguered couple. "Even though it was a vacation, it was the best thing I could have done to keep me up and walking," Amy said later. "I wasn't going to be sitting around in Hawaii."

Home

Remarkably, with the help of her dedicated physical therapists and the support of her loving family, Amy was able to return home. She was fully functioning, with no assistive devices, just ten months after her stroke! Although her dance career was curtailed, she has been able to lead a relatively normal life except for occasional bouts of dizziness, headaches, and some difficulty sleeping. Her local neurologist in Kansas City said it is difficult to believe she ever had a stroke.

As I was preparing this book, I contacted Amy to see if she and her family would meet with me to reflect on all of the events surrounding her stroke and how that crisis had changed their lives over the past three years. Amy and her family graciously agreed to an interview in her home just south of Kansas City.

Hal and I made the trip to Kansas on Saturday, August 10, 2013. We were greeted affectionately by Amy and Jonny and both sets of parents, Dinah and David Wooddell and Sue and Bruce Gardner. Seeing Amy for the first time in several years, I detected no outward signs of any obvious neurologic deficits as a result of her previous stroke. She was very talkative and smiling as she moved around the kitchen to prepare our lunch and bake cookies. She told us how excited she was to be helping others now that she had entered training as a physical therapy assistant.

At that moment, it was difficult for me to remember just how sick she had been. When I voiced this sentiment, Amy's father was quick to answer. He said the main thing that had changed after the stroke was Amy's personality. "Before the stroke," he said, "Amy was very quiet and reserved. But not now. She speaks her mind very quickly and let's me have it if I say something she doesn't like. She would never have done that before!"

Hal and I and the families had a wonderful time of fellowship over a tasty meal. Then I interviewed each couple separately, at Amy and Jonny's request, so I could get a more accurate picture of how each person experienced Amy's illness and what impact it had on each of their lives.

The overwhelming theme each couple expressed was one of being thankful to God and trusting in him completely, especially in the darkest hour of their lives. In retrospect, they could see the hand of God at work providing for them in ways they could not previously have imagined.

Jonny said the first miracle was that Amy's mother, who recognized the signs of a stroke, was with her when she became ill. He said he would probably have been unaware of how serious Amy's situation was and might have delayed her life-saving treatment. He also said despite all of the hardships they had endured, he would not change anything because he knew they were right where God wanted them to be.

Amy said she never questioned why this catastrophe had befallen her. She was thankful she'd had so many years to pursue her love of dancing, but she accepted that God has given her a new path to follow. She said she also recognized how important it was to have her therapist Preeti, who pushed her so hard to gain a full recovery. She said she wants to use her own experience to help others in exactly the way she was helped.

David and Dinah could see how God used all the right people to help throughout the ordeal. First of all, they recognized Amy could not have been in a better location, just a short distance from a renowned medical center, when she needed the most expert medical care available. They had nothing but praise for the interventional radiologist who performed the initial stroke treatment for Amy. They also recounted how God worked through friends and acquaintances to provide physical and spiritual support each and every day.

Sue and Bruce were so thankful to the management and staff at the downtown Marriott Hotel in Washington, D.C., for graciously allowing them to stay there for half price for as long as they needed, for providing free meals, and for all of their acts of kindness and love.

National Orange Popsicle Week

As our time together was drawing to a close, I asked Amy and Jonny to explain the National Orange Popsicle Week (NOPW). I had seen Internet postings from Amy about NOPW for the last year. Amy related again the story about the popsicles. When she was recovering from her stroke, she said, she could not eat any solid foods until she passed a swallow test. During that unwanted fast, she had a craving for orange popsicles. After she passed her swallow test in Chicago, she happily gorged herself on a box of them.

The moment was a powerful one for Amy, one she talked about with her family and friends whenever she told of her ordeal. One day her sister-in-law, Allison, told Amy to think about having an Orange Popsicle Day on the first anniversary of her recovery to commemorate that special event. Amy loved the idea, so in 2011, Amy and Jonny invited about fourteen close friends to their home to share in the small, informal celebration of Amy's recovery from her stroke the year before.

The following year, in 2012, Amy and Jonny decided to have a week celebration instead of only a single day. The theme was initially the same as before, celebrating Amy's recovery from a stroke. The focus of the event this time, however, was to raise awareness of stroke in young people.

A friend of Jonny's told him about a friend of his named Chris, whose 31-year-old wife, Alison, suffered a brainstem stroke similar to what Amy had. Alison was able to communicate with slight head nods, thumb and toe movement, and eye blinks. She was doing rehab; however, it was a marathon, not a sprint. Jonny began spending time with Chris, sharing his experiences and his faith with him in hopes of easing his burdens and encouraging him.

That relationship continued to grow, and it led to Amy becoming involved with Alison in a similar fashion. Amy knew exactly what Alison was thinking and feeling because she had been there before. Not long after, Amy and Jonny asked Chris and Alison to join them on the board of their new organization. It was Alison who came up with the tag line for National Orange Popsicle Week (NOPW), "Raising Awareness of Stroke in Young People."

Alison, who is very intelligent and can communicate by blinking, works through NOPW to raise the awareness of the early signs of stroke, especially in younger people. Strokes are frequently misdiagnosed initially, often with devastating consequences. Alison is living proof.

In 2013, NOPW was celebrated in multiple sites across the country as a result of the organization's use of social media to spread and grow the event. The organization is considering becoming a 501(c)(3) nonprofit entity in the near future. Plans are being made to rebrand the organization as National Orange Popsicle Network, building a community of young stroke victims.

"The popsicle," Jonny said, "is a symbol not necessarily of recovery but of hope."

Our loving God took what looked like a meaningless and tragic event in Amy's life and is using it to help others and to bring him glory. Romans 8:28 says, "And we know that in all things God works for the good of those who love him, who have been called according to his purpose." Grace on Wings was able to play a small part in this still unfolding story and a new ministry.

13

Trusting The Lord To Provide
("Well, Sort Of")

From the very inception of Grace on Wings, God has provided faithfully for all our needs. We have witnessed his faithfulness in providing a wonderful aircraft, dedicated volunteers, prayer warriors, and financial supporters. Although the establishment of a broad base of monthly donors to expand the ministry to the next stage has not yet materialized, God continually amazes us by bringing unanticipated donations when they were most needed.

Engine Upgrade

By the summer of 2010, we were facing a formidable obstacle to the continuation of our ministry. We knew when we purchased our MU-2 aircraft we would need to replace both of the engines when they each amassed a total of 6,000 hours of flight time. By August, only 150 hours remained. The estimated cost to acquire and install the new engines was approximately $600,000.

Hal had been in discussions with representatives from Mitsubishi, Honeywell, and Intercontinental Jet for several years to obtain their assistance in the replacement of our older, less efficient Dash 06 engines with more powerful Dash 10AV engines. This modification would allow Nellie to fly with greater fuel efficiency at a higher altitude and at a greater speed, thus shortening the time of transport for our patients. No one questioned what needed to be done. The only question was how were we going to come up with the massive amount of money to pay for it.

In September 2010, just before our engines timed out, Hal made an arrangement with Mitsubishi, Honeywell, and Intercontinental Jet to update Nellie with new Dash 10AV engines. Each company agreed to donate a significant portion of its costs in support of our ministry, resulting in a donation of $125,000 in parts and services. The Farmers Bank reaffirmed their relationship with us by repackaging our existing debt from the purchase of Nellie with the money still needed to acquire the new engines. They even offered the combined loan at a lower interest rate!

Once again we praised God and thanked all of the people he had brought to us to keep Grace on Wings viable. Our friends at Intercontinental Jet worked to make the engine upgrade quickly and efficiently so there would be minimal impact on our mission schedule. God's faithful provision was apparent to everyone involved in the ministry and to the watching world.

Leap Of Faith

Another issue besides aircraft engine upgrade had become a cause for concern for the ministry. Hal put it in words one morning later in the fall of 2010 as we were sitting in the office drinking coffee and reflecting on the future of the ministry.

"You know, Jim, you've been telling me for about a year that I should stop my job assisting in surgery at Methodist Sports Medicine and devote all of my time to this ministry." He paused to show me the pay stub in his hand, which showed what he had received for all of 2010 for being available two days each week as a surgical physician's assistant.

"Hal, I believe this ministry needs you available on a full-time basis in order to grow," I said, glad for the chance to talk about the issue. "I'd like to ask the board to increase your hours here to full-time and provide for the amount on this pay stub."

When Grace on Wings began, Hal was working in surgery four or five days a week and volunteering all of his spare time to the ministry. As the ministry grew and its demands substantially increased, taking Hal more and more away from his hours of regular employment and his family, the board recognized he needed to be compensated for the essential duties he was performing and his personal loss of income due to it.

Because he was our chief pilot and had to fly every mission, we were forced to turn down some requests because he was in surgery on the days the patients needed to be transported. If he were available to fly at any time and we could do more patient transports, the ministry could make up for the income Hal would lose by quitting his other job.

"I know I need to go full time in ministry," Hal said, "but I haven't been willing to take a final, giant leap of faith and give up my old way of life completely. I think I'm still somewhat afraid of what would happen if Grace on Wings failed and I had no job to return to."

We prayed for wisdom and discernment for Hal that day. Faith *and* action, we knew, were required to keep following God as he led us into deeper relationship with him.

At the next board meeting, Hal shared what God had placed on his heart, that it was time for him to be full time in the ministry. We unanimously endorsed Hal's decision, and we praised God for continuing to bless Grace on Wings. On January 1, 2011, Hal took the leap of faith, trusting completely in God's provision, and began full-time work as CEO and Chief Pilot.

I noticed an overwhelming sense of peace and joy in Hal throughout the spring of 2011. He was finally free to fully engage in all of the innumerable duties involved with operating the ministry. He was able to accept more patient flight requests, make more speaking engagements, handle the day-to-day office chores, and most importantly, share Christ's love with more patients and their families as the number of flights dramatically increased.

Why are Christians amazed when God blesses us as we obey his leading and commands? Why are we surprised when God answers our prayers? It's our human nature, I guess, our continual need to see God at work with our own eyes to bolster our faith.

Grace on Wings is a classic story of ordinary people being called by God for a specific purpose, resulting in a spiritual journey of deeper faith as they step out in obedience to his call. It is by God's grace alone that we are able to answer his call and do what he calls us to do.

Tami's Turn

As the number of mission requests increased, Tami's workload with Grace on Wings grew exponentially. Even so, she continued to work full-time as a physician's assistant in a local emergency room. Her step of faith had not been made apparent to her yet.

In her position as Mission Coordinator for Grace on Wings, Tami was responsible for communicating with patients, families, hospital personnel, and others to arrange for the proposed transports. This work frequently required multiple phone calls and extensive discussions with all of the involved parties in order to make the necessary arrangements. Additionally, Tami had to contact the medical volunteers to arrange the staffing for each flight.

I knew from experience how demanding it was to work in a busy emergency room, and I could see Tami becoming physically and emotionally exhausted from her excessive responsibilities. The ever-present smile and the compassion for others I had witnessed when she and I first met six years before had become casualties of the frenetic lifestyle she was trying desperately to maintain.

The board recognized the need to make Tami a full-time employee, allowing her to concentrate all of her time in ministry. Also, we knew such a move would give Hal and Tami more time to spend together with their family, time that had been taken away by the demands of the growing ministry, time that was essential to their spiritual and emotional well-being. Once again, we trusted God to provide the resources, knowing he is always faithful.

On July 1, 2011, Tami quit her ER job and devoted all of her time and talents to the ministry she had formed with Hal nearly five years before. For her it was a leap of faith, just as it had been for Hal.

Within a few weeks, Tami showed the same sense of inner peace and joy I had seen in Hal a few months before. The ever-present smile that had characterized her returned, and she was eager to immerse herself in the ministry in ways only she could. We all knew we had done the right thing—the godly thing—for Hal and Tami, for Grace on Wings, and for the patients we served.

Hal and Tami increasingly were being praised by everyone who became acquainted with the work they were doing. In every instance, however, they were quick to point to the cross and give God all the glory for allowing them the privilege of serving others in his name.

Marie's Story

Later that month, Tami received a call from Wynn Walent, Assistant National Director of Nos Petits Freres et Soeurs (NPFS). This organization provided aid to needy children in the poorest countries of the world, including Haiti. Wynn asked Grace on Wings to transport a 16-year-old Haitian girl to the Mayo Clinic in Rochester, Minnesota, for a critical surgical procedure.

Grace on Wings, Tami explained, did not fly internationally. If the patient could be flown into the United States, however, we could transport her to the Mayo Clinic. As plans were being discussed, Tami and I learned the horrific story of the young Haitian girl.

Marie was living in her family's severely damaged home following the catastrophic, magnitude 7.0 earthquake that devastated Haiti on January 12, 2010. This massive earthquake had killed an estimated 220,000 people, injured another 300,000, and affected in some way a total of 3,500,000. The family was slowly rebuilding their home over a year later.

The structure, which housed eight people, was little more than a shelter from the elements. The family had very little resources with which to rebuild, so construction was done with cheap concrete and poor quality materials. A plastic tarp functioned as a roof.

One day a storm arose as Marie was sitting inside her home studying for her final exams at school. Beside Marie sat her 3-year-old brother. As the storm intensified, the tarp, acting more like a sail than a roof, caught hold of a sudden gust of wind and caused the concrete wall to begin to collapse inward.

Marie saw what was happening and lunged to cover her little brother from the impending disaster. The full weight of heavy cement blocks from the disintegrating wall struck Marie in the lower back, crushing several vertebrae. Fortunately, her little brother was uninjured.

The family did not know how to deal with this new tragedy. Paralyzed from the waist down, Marie was forced to suffer through the night, exposed to the relentless rainfall and in excruciating pain. The following day, she was loaded into the back of a truck and taken to a local hospital for evaluation.

Medical care in Haiti was primitive by U.S. standards even before the 2010 earthquake. The healthcare system was continually overwhelmed by outbreaks of cholera and other infectious diseases as well as traumatic injuries such as Marie had suffered. Consequently, Marie lay in a bed at the primitive hospital for two days with no testing performed and no treatment rendered.

When attention could finally be given to her situation, Marie was transferred to a larger hospital in the capital city of Port au Prince. In Port au Prince she received X-rays showing severe fractures to the T-12 and L-1 vertebrae. The bone fragments from the fractures were severely displaced and had damaged her spinal cord, causing paralysis from the waist down.

A team of doctors from the Mayo Clinic was working in the hospital at the time. They knew Marie needed surgery to stabilize her broken back and hopefully restore some neurologic function by taking the pressure off of the spinal cord. The Mayo Clinic and their physicians graciously offered to donate their services for Marie's care if she could find a way to get to Mayo's home facility in Minnesota.

International air ambulance flights are very expensive, sometimes more than $100,000, when contracting with a commercial carrier. With no insurance and no money for the flight and other expenses she would incur, Marie was a world away from the expert medical care she so desperately needed. The missionary relief workers in

Haiti were moved by Marie's predicament and began to search for a way to get her to the United States.

Wynn Walent, the man who called Tami, told her he had discovered a Christian organization named Missionary Flights International (MFI) based in Ft. Pierce, Florida. They had been flying DC-3 cargo flights to and from Haiti several times each week since the earthquake. The organization had generously agreed to donate their services to fly Marie to Florida on a cot secured to the floor of their DC-3 aircraft. Then Grace on Wings would complete Marie's long and painful journey to the Mayo Clinic in Minnesota.

Through The Storm

In planning the mission, Hal had a multitude of factors to consider. First, he had to coordinate a timely transfer of Marie at MFI's home base in Florida. Since the MFI flight from Haiti would take three and a half hours and could only be performed during the daytime, Grace on Wings would have to be in Florida by mid-afternoon to meet the MFI crew. The flight from Indianapolis to Ft. Pierce was approximately three and a half hours. The weather forecast on the projected flight date called for thunderstorms scattered throughout the flight path all the way from Florida to Minnesota.

Next, Hal had to plan for a fuel stop in Indianapolis during the five-hour flight from Florida to the Mayo Clinic in Rochester, Minnesota. With severe storms to contend with, he had to plan for the contingency of deviating from the intended flight plan and going around the storms, if necessary. Any deviation from the filed flight plan would affect the amount of fuel needed and also the timing of the mission.

Finally, Hal knew the Rochester airport tower closed at 11 p.m., so he had to make sure Grace on Wings landed before the tower closed for the night. Otherwise, he would have to land at another controlled airfield, which would delay getting Marie to the Mayo Clinic as planned.

On the afternoon of July 28, 2011, we landed at the MFI base in Ft. Pierce, Florida, on schedule. The deep blue skies showed no hint of any thunderstorm activity so common along the Atlantic coastline that time of year. We found our patient, Marie, lying on a makeshift cot secured to the bare metal floor of the DC-3 cargo plane normally used to carry lifesaving supplies to Haiti.

Marie, who spoke no English, was clutching a Bible, translated into her native Creole language, firmly to her chest. Marie's mother was at her side and greeted us warmly. Wynn, the missionary who had arranged for Marie's flight, was also with Marie and served as interpreter for her and her mother.

Our medical team assessed Marie and carefully transferred her to our customized cot system. Before we loaded her onto our aircraft, the MFI personnel joined the Grace on Wings crew in praying over Marie. We asked God to heal her and provide for all her needs during this crisis.

Once aboard Nellie, the crew placed headphones on Marie so she could listen to Christian music during the long northbound flight. A large smile broke out on her face. Through Wynn, her interpreter, she told the crew she loved music and loved to sing.

As the medical crew attended to Marie and her mother, Hal was busy dodging the gathering thunderstorms in the Midwest. Flashes of lightning could be seen in the thunderclouds towering above the aircraft in the distance as we entered the airspace over southeastern Minnesota. Hal knew the Rochester tower would soon be closing for the night, and he was anxiously waiting for their radio call to begin his descent.

"Medevac 910 November Foxtrot, this is Rochester approach."

"Rochester, this is Medevac 910 November Foxtrot," Hal replied.

Just in time and through the storm, Rochester approach handed us off to the tower for the landing at the appropriate time. Then, as a final challenge after an extremely long day of flying, Hal had to deal with a dense fog moving in to envelope the airfield just as he was on final approach.

By God's grace, Hal got Nellie on the ground safely before the tower closed for the night. The medical crew then transported Marie to the Mayo Clinic. There they tucked her into her hospital bed to await the scheduled surgery on her crushed vertebrae.

As we flew back to our home base in Indianapolis, we were exhausted after a very long day of flying from one end of the country to the other. We were thankful for the opportunity to serve Marie. We recognized, however, the tremendous challenges she still faced in her recovery from such a devastating injury. As was typical of our operations, we would maintain contact with her if at all possible.

His Way Of Grace

Two years later, in August of 2013, I received the following message in an email from Wynn Walent regarding Marie's current status.

Marie is doing well. We built a house for her and her family, and she is going to school as well. She is still in a wheelchair, of course, but seems very positive when I see her, which is frequently.

I thought to myself, she seems very positive. How could an innocent young girl, living in one of the poorest countries on the face of the earth, paralyzed from the waist down through no fault of her own, be positive about anything? How could our loving God allow such suffering to occur? And would I be able to stand firm in my faith if such a disaster afflicted me?

It was not the first time such thoughts had entered my mind. So many of the patients I'd seen in the ER or on our flights had similar stories of unimaginable pain and suffering, both physically and emotionally. It was difficult for me to understand how people could possibly successfully navigate those treacherous waters of life without a firm belief in God. I would be consumed with anger, resentment, bitterness, and self-pity if I were to see my situation solely through the lens of human existence.

Even Job, who God himself described as blameless and upright, became distraught from the many severe trials he faced. At one point, he cursed the day of his birth. But then God set the record straight for Job and for the rest of his creation. In Job 38:4, God says to Job, "Where were you when I laid the earth's foundation?" For the next four chapters, God rebukes Job for questioning his sovereignty.

Having been humbled by the testimony of all mighty God, Job responds in Job 42:5–6, "My ears had heard of you but now my eyes have seen you. Therefore I despise myself and repent in dust and ashes."

Sometimes we can question the usefulness of our efforts if we focus only on results others deem worthy or successful. But we can be comforted in knowing God does not expect us to heal every person we serve. He does, however, expect us to show up and use all of the gifts and talents he has bestowed upon us to help those in need. The results are in God's domain, but the work is ours. It is his way of grace.

Why does God allow some to suffer while others seem to go through life unscathed by tragedy? Why are some healed while others remain trapped within a permanently damaged body? I don't have the answers to those age-old questions. But I know one day all things will be revealed to us when Jesus returns to establish his kingdom here on earth.

Until then, we need to trust God in all things, even when it seems circumstances make no earthly sense. In Isaiah 55:8–9 God says, "For my thoughts are not your thoughts, neither are your ways my ways ... As the heavens are higher than the earth, so are my ways higher than your ways and my thoughts than your thoughts."

14

Sheltered From The Storm
("Life Is Like A ... ")

"I have a philosophy that goes like this. Life is like one of those bumper car rides you took when you were a kid. When you bump into something in life, you can hold the wheel and waste your ride, or you can turn the wheel and something else will happen. Get on with life and go in another direction."

These were the words of Ken Cummins when I talked with him about two years after Grace on Wings transported him from Maryland to Illinois after an accident. Ken sustained serious injuries while helping victims of one of the worst hurricane disasters in our country's history. He, in turn, needed help.

His words surprised and challenged me. What metaphor did I have about life? Was it a bumper car ride, a walk in a forest, a long-distance marathon, an unexpected storm, or what?

Ken's Story

Hurricane Irene struck the East Coast of the United States during late August 2011, causing widespread destruction of property and disruption of vital services to the region. Along with many other humanitarian organizations, the Federal Emergency Management Agency (FEMA) immediately went into action.

FEMA often calls on disaster relief agencies to assist in their efforts to help victims of tragedies such as hurricanes, earthquakes, tornadoes, flooding, and the like. One such entity is the Illinois Baptist State Association (IBSA) Disaster Relief. It is comprised of 1,500 volunteers from all over the state who are committed to sharing the hope of Jesus with those whose lives have been impacted by disasters.

Ken Cummins, a retired teacher and wrestling coach from Plano, Illinois, had been leading teams of volunteer relief workers for IBSA for nearly six years when Hurricane Irene hit. He previously had been involved in extensive cleanup operations following Hurricane Katrina in Bogalusa, Louisiana, and other local disaster relief efforts. In September 2011, Ken was asked to lead a team to the badly damaged community of Leonardtown, Maryland, to clear fallen trees as a result of Hurricane Irene.

Ken's team specialized in using chainsaws to remove damaged trees and clear the debris in a safe manner. On Wednesday, September 14, Ken's crew began their third day of work as usual. That day would turn out to be anything but usual for Ken.

I had seen the medical reports describing Ken's injuries at the time I approved his medical evacuation flight by Grace on Wings two years before. But I wanted to hear from Ken and his wife, Pam, just how their lives were impacted by the events on that fateful day.

"Ken, tell me in your own words what happened to you in Maryland," I said. I listened in awe as his retelling of that day unfolded.

"Well, I spotted a huge tree limb about twenty-three feet above the ground that needed to be cut down," he began. "I set a ladder against the trunk of the tree and climbed to the top of the ladder. You know, I'm a state chainsaw trainer, so this was just business as usual for me.

"I reached out with the chain saw and made several cuts in the tree limb. As soon as I made the last cut through the limb, it broke funny on me and peeled me and the ladder off the tree."

"Were you knocked out during the fall to the ground?" I asked.

"I never was unconscious. I rode the ladder down and landed hard on my left side. Thank God I didn't hit my head or break my neck. But I did break five ribs on the left side and two ribs on the right side, and I fractured three vertebrae in my back.

"It all happened so fast. I remember my team members all gathered around and telling me it was going to be okay. Then I was flown to Prince George Hospital in a Maryland State Police helicopter."

"Pam, where were you when you first heard about Ken's accident?" I asked.

"I was back home in Illinois when the hospital and Ken's team members notified me. I didn't know how bad things were for several days. Ken was injured on a Wednesday, and we had another IBSA Disaster Relief Team from Northern Illinois getting ready to go on Sunday. I decided to drive my car and go with the team to Maryland. But I was not comfortable driving at night. Fortunately, God provided for me throughout the crisis."

"How did you see God at work?" I asked.

"A chaplain friend of ours, Ed, was going to Maryland with the relief team on Sunday. When he heard about my needs, he volunteered to help me make the long drive. He was such a blessing to me. He listened and comforted me as we talked about Ken's situation. I felt God had provided an answer to my prayers through him.

"Ed said he did wonder why God had allowed this to happen to Ken. But I said, 'There is somebody in that hospital he wants Ken to talk to. Who it is, I don't know.'"

"When Pam walked into my room at the hospital, I said, 'You're my lifeline!'" Ken said.

Pam continued. "My place was there with Ken. For the next two weeks I spent my time in the hospital or in the hotel. Again, God provided for me in a big way."

"How was that?" I asked.

"Ken's team gave me support like a family, but when their work was finished, they had to return home. A team member named Gladys, a widow who had made her first trip with Ken's team, offered to stay with me and provide support during the rest of the time Ken was hospitalized in Maryland. I don't know what I would have done without her. She even drove my car back to Illinois while I flew home with Ken on Grace on Wings," Pam said.

"Ken, how did you do after you got to the hospital?" I asked.

"Well, I was in a lot of pain and I did have some complications. At one point, the surgeons had to open up my chest and drain a lot of blood from around my lungs. I think I was given a transfusion of eight units of blood. After that, the main problem was just dealing with all of the pain from the broken bones.

"In the hospital, I prayed for God's grace, not much else. I never questioned any of it. I never said, 'Why me?' When you ask that question, you're almost saying it would be okay if it happened to someone else."

"Where did your strong faith come from?" I asked.

"I was led to the Lord by my Sunday school teacher, Elvin, when I was thirteen years old. Since then I've been a part of the Baptist church and tried to live like the Bible says. It's just by God's grace I was able to be strong," Ken said.

Just By God's Grace

His statement about God's grace touched me deeply. All that we did through Grace on Wings was because of God's grace, through God's grace. None of it was us.

"Fred, one of my team members, told us about Grace on Wings," Ken continued. "He said we might be able to get you to fly me back to Illinois. That's how Grace on Wings came into the story. My daughter-in-law, a nurse at Carle Clinic in Champaign, Illinois, lined up my transfer to Champaign for rehab when I was ready to go from the hospital in Maryland."

"I knew when I heard the name *Grace on Wings* it was how we were supposed to get Ken home," Pam said. "It was such a comfort having you guys there to take good care of Ken and to pray over him."

"I understand I was mission #151 for Grace on Wings and the first flight you made for someone with chest tubes coming out of him," Ken said. "I remember talking with Tami all the way."

"Ken, tell me how God used you to witness to others through your crisis," I said.

"You know, I asked everybody at that hospital if they were a Christian. I think non-believers have a hard time with the confidence believers have. I never complained. I didn't want to be a burden to anybody. I knew I was lucky to be alive.

"God had a plan in all that happened. I've had an opportunity to share my testimony with people almost every day over the last two years."

"So, did you retire from the disaster relief work after your accident?" I asked.

"There are two words that I've never seen in the Bible—retirement and vacation," Ken said and laughed.

"Are you still climbing trees and leading chain saw teams?" I asked.

"Oh, yes. I'll keep doing it as long as I can. You don't retire from being a Christian," he said.

"What advice would you give other people who may be going through a terrible crisis in their life?" I asked.

"I tell people, when you bump into a crisis, just turn your wheel and get on with life. Don't waste your ride. It's the only one you get," he said.

Sometimes, as in Ken's situation, by God's grace, recovery comes fairly quickly. In those cases, we can turn our wheel and move on with our life. Other times, a tragedy can occur with more far-reaching and long-lasting consequences. Then it becomes necessary to adjust our lives to the "new normal" we are faced with. Such was the case for the family of Eric Berry when Grace on Wings answered their call for help.

Eric's Story

As I parked in front of the Berry's home, I saw Brian waving to me from the front porch. Brian, Eric's father, was busily working a small leaf blower to clear the porch and sidewalk on that beautiful fall day. The house appeared well kept and fit the mature, working class neighborhood on the south side of Indianapolis where it was located. Walking up to the house, I suddenly realized Eric and his family lived within a half mile of where Grace on Wings held its Gala event each year on the campus of the University of Indianapolis.

"Hi, Jim. I see you found it," Brian said. He and his wife, Brenda, had invited me to their home to hear Eric's story. The small part of Eric's story I knew related to the medical reports I had reviewed before approving his emergency transport more than three years before. I would soon learn the rest of the story.

"Hi, Brian. I had no idea you lived so close to the university," I replied.

"Yes, it's close enough we can walk Eric to the Grace on Wings Gala in his wheelchair if the weather is decent."

"It was great seeing Eric with your family and friends at the hog roast last weekend, I said. "I loved your T-shirts."

Grace on Wings had held its 7th Annual Aviation Festival and Hog Roast just a week before. Eric's family had special T-shirts made for the occasion. All of his family, friends, and caregivers sported a gray tee shirt with the Grace on Wings logo on the front. But the most prominent feature on the shirt was "Mission #66, Eric Berry, February 4, 2010" in bright purple on the front and back.

"It's become our mission to make people aware of Grace on Wings," Brian said, smiling in response to my comment about the shirts.

"We had a lot of people ask about Eric because of those shirts. It gave us a chance to tell them about what Grace on Wings did for us," he added. "Come on in, and we'll say hi to Eric."

We entered the living room and then passed through an enlarged doorway into Eric's room on the first floor of the house. Eric was there, resting comfortably it seemed in his specialized hospital bed.

"This was Eric's room when he was growing up," Brian said.

"Hi Eric," I said. "It's good to see you again."

Eric was unable to speak, but he was very alert and aware of my presence. I looked around the room and saw the walls adorned with pictures of Eric taken on various occasions with friends and family before his tragedy three and a half years ago. The pictures revealed a very handsome young man with a winsome smile. He appeared carefree and full of life.

Brenda, Eric's mother, stood beside the bed, lovingly caressing Eric's face. "Eric, this is Dr. Milstead. He helped get you home on Grace on Wings after your stroke."

She followed my gaze and said, "Eric had a lot of friends. He was always smiling and everyone loved him. We're waiting for that beautiful smile to come back one day."

"I wish I could forget what his breathing sounded like when I found him, but I never will," Brian said as he fought back tears, remembering that day. "He was just barely clinging to life."

"Why don't we go sit in the dining room where we can talk?" Brenda said. "You can tell Jim the whole story in there."

Eric's room opened up into an expanded bathroom with a handicap accessible shower and a lift device. As we passed through it on the way to the dining room, I said, "It looks like you have done a lot of remodeling here."

"A good friend helped me remodel the house to make Eric as comfortable as possible," Brian said as we sat down at the dining room table. "It had to be done. We never considered any option for Eric except bringing him home to take care of him the best we could. A lot of people were concerned it would be more than we could handle. But I remembered the Bible said God wouldn't give us more than we could bear. So, this is our new normal."

"Would you like something to drink, Jim?" Brenda asked.

"Iced tea would be good if you have it," I said, already amazed but ready for the rest of the story.

"Is sweetened tea ok?"

"That's perfect, thank you."

When Brenda returned with the tea, I explained the purpose for my visit. "I'm writing a book about Grace on Wings, and I would like to tell Eric's story, your family's story, so others who are suffering from a similar tragedy can find hope in their time of despair. I know the medical facts about Eric's case, but there is so much more I don't know. Tell me what happened in your words and how your life has been impacted."

I could tell Brian was pleased with the request. He launched immediately into the story.

An Unexpected Storm

"Eric moved to Chicago in 2006," Brian began. "He was thirty-two at the time. He loved living in downtown Chicago, and he had tons of friends. He worked as a graphic designer for Westdale Asset Management, a company that owned apartment complexes. His job was to design and help renovate the complexes. Not long before his stroke, Eric moved into an apartment in the western suburb of Westmont, where he managed 2,200 apartments. He was a hard worker, and his boss loved him.

"Eric was supposed to be part of a conference call that included his boss, Barbara, at 2 p.m. on January 12, 2010. The call went on without him. After the call was over, his boss called my wife, Brenda, and said she was worried about Eric because he didn't show up at work that day. By then it was 4:30 p.m."

"Eric had been having some headaches, so his coworkers just thought he might be taking a day off," Brenda said.

"Brenda tried to reach Eric by calling his apartment but got no answer. She knew I was in Chicago on business, so she called me and told me to check on Eric in person. We both knew something was wrong because it wasn't like Eric to miss work. Ten minutes later I'm kicking down his apartment door.

"I found Eric on the couch, unresponsive and barely alive," Brian said. "He was gasping for each breath. That's the sound I can't get out of my mind.

"I called 911, and the paramedics came and took him to the Good Samaritan Hospital in Downer's Grove. There the doctors told me he had had a hemorrhage in his brain and would need neurosurgery right away. They would need to take off the left half of his skull to drain the blood and stop the bleeding. Even then, they said he might not live."

As Medical Director for Grace on Wings, I knew from his medical records Eric had a ruptured arteriovenous malformation (AVM) in the left frontal lobe of his brain. He had initial surgery at Good Samaritan Hospital and then was transferred to the University of Illinois Chicago (UIC) Hospital for more specialized neurologic treatment. He remained there for nearly three weeks.

"Megan set up a CaringBridge website for Eric during that time," Brenda said, picking up the story from Brian. "She turned out to be our go-to person, our control center, if you will."

"Who is Megan?" I asked.

"Megan is Michael's wife, Eric's sister-in-law," she said. "Michael loves his older brother."

"The first piece of good news came when the doctors said we could take our son back to Indianapolis in a day or two," Brian said. "They told us to start making arrangements to get him to a facility in Indianapolis that could take care of him. But how would we do that? The social worker said we could get an ambulance to transfer Eric from Chicago to Indianapolis for about $3,000. Having driven I-65 between Indianapolis and Chicago a few thousand times, I knew I couldn't put Eric in an ambulance and bump down the road for four hours when he was still recovering from a severe brain injury."

"That's when Megan told us about Grace on Wings," Brenda said. "We had never heard of your ministry before then. But Megan searched the Internet for air ambulances, and your website came up. She called, and Hal answered right away. He said Grace on Wings could get Eric back to Indianapolis the next day. Megan was ecstatic when Hal said it would only take thirty-three minutes flying time and cost only $1,500!"

"We made arrangements for Eric to be admitted to a long-term, acute care hospital near our home," Brian said. "Brenda and I met Tami and the medical crew for the first time when they delivered Eric to Kindred South Hospital in Greenwood, Indiana, late at night on February 4, 2010."

"Megan took a picture of the Grace on Wings medic, Todd, as the crew arrived with Eric," Brenda said. "In the picture, you can see a distinct halo around the cross on the logo on the back of his flight suit."

"Eric flew with Grace on Wings on a Thursday," Brian said. "That next Sunday, Hal and Tami stopped by to visit us at the hospital in Greenwood and to pray over Eric. That was the first time we met Hal. I can't tell you how much that visit meant to us. We could tell Eric wasn't just a flight to them.

"Hal and Tami came to see Eric several times after that time. Hal even asked me to speak at the 2010 Gala. We did go to the gala, but it was too soon to talk about what had happened.

"Eric was in Kindred South Hospital for a few months, and then he was admitted into a nursing home as a temporary measure. We remodeled the house during that time to get ready for when we could get Eric home with us again.

"He was at the nursing home for one year and received great care there. We brought Eric home on May 26, 2011. His nurse, Claire Fullenkamp, liked working with Eric so much she started working for Tender Care home health care agency so she could take care of him at home."

"Hal and Tami came to Eric's Open House," Brenda said. "Having Hal and Tami choose to stay in touch with us really means a lot. Now Brian keeps Hal supplied with the spicy barbecue sauce he likes," she said and laughed.

"I know Hal likes spicy food," I said and joined her laugh. "What's the name of the sauce you get him?"

"It's called Vinegar and Pepper, and I buy it at Jungle Jim's International Market in Cincinnati. It's the hottest barbecue sauce I've found, and Hal loves it."

"How are you dealing with the challenges you've faced since Eric's stroke?" I asked.

"It's what God handed us to deal with, and we adjust our life to make Eric as comfortable as we can," Brian said. "We don't know where this is going to lead us, but we're going down the path with him."

"When Eric was in the nursing home, we watched and learned and asked a lot of questions," Brenda said. "It's not easy, but it's our new lifestyle."

"We've been married forty-four years," Brian said. "We knew without even talking about it we were going to bring Eric home."

Miracles Happen

"We don't give up hope," Brenda said. "Eric has changed so much in the last two months. His nurses and the physical therapists have all seen it. He still doesn't speak, but he is becoming a lot more vocal, and he makes purposeful movements. He lets you know when he's had enough therapy. He makes a noise and pulls away. He's never done that before. He focuses on us more now too. Eric is changing."

"Tell Jim how Eric reacted to one of Bernie's jokes not long ago," Brian said. "Bernie is one of Eric's home health nurses, and he's a real jokester."

"Well, we'd never heard Eric laugh since his stroke," Brenda said. "Eric used to laugh all the time. Bernie comes in to take care of Eric every Saturday and always greets Eric by saying, 'Good morning, my friend.' He then tells Eric about the weather and whatever is going on in his life. That morning Bernie said, 'I may have lost my mind, Eric. I'm thinking about buying a pocket puppy at a store in Chicago, near Lincoln Park. When I walked into the store, I saw what I thought was a beanie baby puppy in a small cage. When that thing moved, I almost wet my pants!'"

"Eric got a smile on his face, and for the first time in three and a half years I heard his wonderful laugh!" Brenda said. "I couldn't believe my ears. Bernie and I stood there, amazed, not wanting it to end. I wish I'd captured it on video so I could play it over and over again."

"Praise God," I said. "That's got to fill you with renewed hope for Eric's recovery. Make sure Bernie keeps telling funny stories."

I glanced at my watch. My time with Eric's family was up. I wanted to get Eric's amazing story written before the end of the day, but I had just one more question. "What advice do you have for others going through difficult times such as yours?"

"Don't give up!" Brian said. "Miracles happen. We'll never give up."

In that moment, I thought again about Ken Cummin's words, "Life is like one of those bumper car rides you took when you were a kid." The unexpected storms happen, but what we do through them is our choice. I was so glad Hal had answered the call, he and Tami had arranged for Eric's flight, and I had this chance to tell Eric's amazing story.

15

Boast Only In The Lord
("I'm A Humble Guy—Oops!")

With new engines, we were ready to fly again. And with both Hal and Tami committed to the ministry full-time, we were positioned for more assignments, more chances to serve the Lord with excellence. And we did so. By the end of the summer of 2012, we had flown 215 missions, transporting patients and family members from points all over the United States. Our work had come to the attention of many people and organizations. Soon we would have an opportunity to discover the answer to a very important question: How can we as Christians best handle praise or success that comes our way so that God is glorified?

The events were set in motion one day in September of 2012 when Hal called me and said, "Jim, you're not going to believe this, brother. Grace on Wings just won an award as the best fixed-wing air ambulance service in the United States!"

Best In The U.S.

The Association of Air Medical Services (AAMS) selects one air ambulance service each year to receive its prestigious award at the annual Air Medical Transport Conference (AMTC) meeting. The award is in recognition of the superior level of patient care, management prowess, quality leadership through visionary and innovative approaches, customer service, safety consciousness, marketing ingenuity, community service, and commitment to the medical transport community as a whole.

Grace on Wings had been a member of AAMS since the inception of our ministry in 2006, and we had been attending the AMTC events each fall. But I didn't consider, and I don't think anyone else on the staff or board did either, the possibility we might receive such a high honor from our colleagues in the medical aviation industry. Instead, we had gradually become more comfortable with our position as a nonprofit volunteer organization in an industry populated with large, for-profit corporations. The award signaled to us we had become accepted and officially recognized by our peers.

"We'll receive the award at a special ceremony on the first night of the AMTC in Seattle," Hal informed me. I could tell by the sound of his voice how excited he was.

"That's awesome," I said. A sense of pride welled up inside me at that moment.

The conference for 2012 was to be held in the convention center in downtown Seattle, Washington. The award ceremony was scheduled for the evening of October 22, 2012. Hal, Tami, and I decided to attend the conference along with two volunteer crewmembers, Matt Guy and Scott Coombs.

Matt, a paramedic and RN, has been instrumental in the growth of the ministry through his dedication to staffing flights and overseeing the training of our medical personnel for several years. Scott, a full-time paramedic, has distinguished himself by volunteering to staff many of our missions and by his unending enthusiasm for the ministry. More importantly, Matt and Scott love the Lord, and the love of Christ radiates from them in their daily lives.

On the evening of the awards ceremony, the five of us were seated strategically at a table near the stage along with others who would be recognized that evening for receiving various coveted industry awards. During the dinner preceding the awards ceremony, I noticed Hal, who would be accepting the award for Grace on Wings, nervously picking at his food and being uncharacteristically silent. I sensed his anxiety had been building throughout the day and was reaching a crescendo just as the award presentations were about to begin.

We watched and eagerly applauded as many individuals and hospital programs were given prestigious awards for their unique contributions to the medical aviation industry. Seated behind Hal, I silently prayed for him to have the strength to witness boldly for Christ when it was finally time for Grace on Wings to be recognized.

Hal had been planning his acceptance speech for nearly a month, and Jesus was to be the centerpiece of his message. Many times I had seen Hal speak to church groups, civic organizations, and large crowds in other venues. He was adept at passionately sharing the story of our ministry. He would talk about how God had worked in our lives as well as in the ministry and the lives of the patients and shared the hope we all have in Jesus Christ.

This ceremony, however, was a secular event in Seattle, a place not typically thought of as a hotbed of evangelism. I didn't know how this crowd would receive the gospel message Hal was about to offer. And I wondered how he would deliver it.

All Glory And Honor To God

As the lights in the auditorium dimmed, the massive video screen to the left of the stage came to life. A moving, two and a half minute documentary film on Grace on Wings captivated the audience. Then, taking our cue, the five of us representing the ministry walked to the stage as the video announced, "This year's Fixed Wing Award of Excellence goes to Grace on Wings!"

I was filled with joy as I watched the video and recalled the long journey that had led us to that moment. Then the massive red cross on the tail of Nellie flashed across the screen, and I silently thanked God for the awesome privilege of being allowed to share in his work. There was no room for pride, only humility. Any success Grace on Wings had achieved was a result of the transforming power of Christ in our lives.

Hal stepped forward tentatively to receive the award from the master of ceremonies. The four of us stood motionless behind him.

He turned to address the audience slowly, offering a heartfelt appreciation to AAMS for the gracious award we had been given.

Then it happened.

Hal will tell you he really can't remember what he said next, but he was sure the Holy Spirit spoke through him. As the audience listened intently, Hal stated that we were humbled to receive such an award but "all of the glory and honor needs to go to our Lord and Savior, Jesus Christ."

There was a polite, somewhat awkward applause as we walked off the stage and regained our seats. I noticed a palpable tension in the room. The Word of God, like a two-edged sword, had pierced many people to their very core.

Later, after the conclusion of the formal ceremonies, a number of attendees came up to us and thanked us for the work we were doing. They identified themselves as fellow Christians and offered precious words of encouragement and appreciation for the boldness with which we presented the gospel.

The following day was flight-suit day, the designated day of the AMTC when all flight crews proudly wore their uniforms while attending the many medical education sessions and organizational business meetings. Even in the midst of thousands of people dressed in a variety of bright colors and designs, Grace on Wings crewmembers were easy to identify. Our black flight suits bearing a large red cross trimmed with a thin white border proclaimed the uniqueness of our ministry. Throughout the day, many more colleagues congratulated us for winning the award and lavished words of praise and encouragement on us for serving people in the name of Jesus.

Feeling a bit uncomfortable because of the newfound attention we had garnered, I was reminded of the apostle Paul's words of wisdom to the Galatians when he said, "May I never boast except in the cross of our Lord Jesus Christ" (Galatians 6:14). I was also challenged to keep our calling foremost. The apostle Paul's words to the church in Philippi offered an important guideline for our conduct.

Do nothing out of selfish ambition or vain conceit, but in humility consider others better than yourselves. Each of you should look not only to your own interests, but also to the interests of others. Your attitude should be the same as that of Christ Jesus: Who, being in very nature God, did not consider equality with God something to be grasped, but made himself nothing, taking the very nature of a servant, being made in human likeness. And being found in appearance as a man, he humbled himself and became obedient to death — even death on a cross! (Philippians 2:3–8)

We were not unaware of the dangers of pride, a sin that could deceptively take hold of us and have us strutting around, patting ourselves on the back, and vainly proclaiming to the world what splendid creatures we are. That is why everyone intimately involved in the Grace on Wings ministry is committed to point to the cross on our logo when people heap on accolades. If the apostle Paul could boast of nothing except the cross of the Lord Jesus Christ, then we had to follow his example and do likewise.

On The Horizon

So where could we go after having such a wonderful, mountaintop experience? Luke 12:48 gave us the answer. "From everyone who has been given much, much will be demanded; and from the one who has been entrusted with much, much more will be asked."

We knew God was not done with us yet. We identified with the lyrics of the song made popular by the Carpenters in the 1970s, "We've Only Just Begun." Hal had said from the beginning, "Grace on Wings is going to continue serving until God puts an end to the ministry or until Jesus returns, whichever comes first." We would continue to walk by faith, one day at a time, as we served more and more patients and made the love of Christ known to all who would listen.

Continuing to grow and distinguish the ministry in its service was our foremost goal. At the same time, we understood the need to take a long-term approach to our operation so there would be someone to carry on the ministry long after we were gone. One day, Hal said, he would be flying a desk instead of an airplane. For Grace on Wings to survive in the future, we needed to have new "missionaries" to carry on the work we started.

The race we run is a marathon, not a sprint. The words in Hebrews 12:1–3 say it better than any of us can.

> Therefore, since we are surrounded by such a great cloud of witnesses, let us throw off everything that hinders and the sin that so easily entangles, and let us run with perseverance the race marked out for us. Let us fix our eyes on Jesus, the author and perfecter of our faith, who for the joy set before him endured the cross, scorning its shame, and sat down at the right hand of the throne of God. Consider him who endured such opposition from sinful men, so that you will not grow weary and lose heart.

So we came down from the mountaintop and got busy doing the day-to-day business of the ministry, faithfully and humbly showing the love of Christ to everyone we met—patients, hospital personnel, aviation employees, donors, volunteers, and the world at large. We kept our eyes fixed on Jesus and the horizon ahead of us.

Our call included serving the whole spectrum of humanity, and by God's grace we were involved with people who were just beginning their lives as well as others who were nearing the end.

Jackson's Story

Jackson W. was unexpectedly born at just twenty-four weeks gestation, sixteen weeks prematurely, at Hancock County Hospital in Greenfield, Indiana. His family was traveling from their home in Buffalo, New York, to visit family in Kansas during spring break from school when the crisis arose. Jackson was initially resuscitated and then transferred to the neonatal intensive care unit at St. Vincent Hospital in Indianapolis, where he was given only a 10 to 20 percent chance of survival.

Seven difficult weeks later, Grace on Wings was contacted to fly Jackson and his mother home to Buffalo to be reunited with the rest of the family.

Jackson's mother, Jennifer, gave the following testimony.

After spending two months in the NICU at St. Vincent Women's Hospital, Jackson had endured three surgeries and countless transfusions and diagnostic tests. He was finally off the ventilator and ready to move closer to home. Unfortunately, our insurance company failed to see the medical necessity of transporting our baby boy closer to home, allowing our family to be reunited and me to return to work.

This is where Grace on Wings stepped in. They are such a blessing! From the second they stepped into the room, a tremendous peace came with them. They took such great care of our little boy and transported him safely to Buffalo. We are forever grateful.

Beckie's Story

In the spring of 2013, Beckie Galbreath was diagnosed with a disease called Amyotrophic Lateral Sclerosis (ALS), a progressive neurodegenerative disease that affects nerve cells in the brain and spinal cord. When Beckie's condition took an unexpected turn for the worse, Grace on Wings answered the call for help.

I was familiar with ALS because of Lou Gehrig, nicknamed "The Iron Horse," a man generally considered one of the greatest baseball players of all time. He was renowned for his prowess as a hitter and for his durability, playing in 2,130 consecutive games. Yet, in my mind, the most powerful image his name conjures up is the scene in Yankee Stadium on July 4, 1939, where Gehrig gave his iconic speech, "The Luckiest Man on the Face of the Earth."

The transcript of the speech is only a few paragraphs long but filled with words of hope and courage. It began, "Fans, for the past two weeks you have been reading about the bad break I got. Yet today I consider myself the luckiest man on the face of this earth." He ends with, "So I close in saying that I may have had a tough break, but I have an awful lot to live for."

Although he died at age thirty-seven of ALS, the manner in which he dealt with the terminal disease is an inspiration to all. Patients with ALS, or "Lou Gehrig's Disease" as it is commonly known, have progressive loss of muscle strength, finally resulting in death when the muscles of respiration cease to function. The strength and courage they display in the face of death, as Lou Gehrig did, provide an example for us as we deal with adversity in our own lives.

In Beckie's case, the ALS was very aggressive. She became dependent on a BiPap machine, a device that delivers pressurized air through a mask to support the patient's breathing. Knowing the end was near, Beckie's husband wanted her to be able to spend the remaining days of her life in the presence of family. Thinking she had some time left before the end, he and Beckie decided to take an RV from their home in Paris, Illinois, to visit relatives in the northwestern part of the state, some 200 miles away from home.

Hal received a call from Beckie's husband, who said she had to be hospitalized in Moline, Illinois, when she was unable to support her breathing even with the assistance of the BiPap machine. She had already decided she did not want any heroic measures taken to sustain her life. She understood interventions such as placing a tube in her airway and putting her on a ventilator would not alter the course of her disease.

"Beckie's only wish," he said, "is to get back home to say her good-byes to her kids and grandkids."

The family had already explored ground transport. They were shocked to discover the cost of an ambulance transport would be more than $8,000 and would take approximately four hours to complete. They were very relieved, however, when Hal said the cost of a 45-minute flight from Galesburg, Illinois, to Terre Haute, Indiana, would be less than $3,000. Tami then set the transfer in motion.

During the transport, Beckie experienced a lot of difficulty breathing. "It was difficult to watch her struggle for each breath," Tami said, "but we were determined to get her home to fulfill her last wish."

Beckie survived the transport and was greeted at the airport by her loving family. She was taken to the Paris Community Hospital, where her husband was employed, and admitted for supportive care in her hometown. She died peacefully the following day.

God's Grace

Unbeknownst to the Grace on Wings crew, Beckie's family in Paris, Illinois, had contacted a local television station, WTHI Channel 10 in Terre Haute, Indiana. They wanted the public to hear about the mission to bring Beckie home to die in the presence of her family. Grace on Wings became the featured story on the broadcast the evening she died.

"God gives us the means to do the mission," Hal said to the reporter who interviewed him. "It is a privilege to serve others in his name."

Grace on Wings received an email from a member of Beckie's family shortly after her death.

> Just want to thank you guys for everything you did for my mother and our family! It was a true blessing to be able to have her flown back home to be with her loved ones. Unfortunately, she passed away early this morning. Without you guys she wouldn't have been able to be here with all of her family and friends. That was all she wanted and you made this possible!
>
> You have no idea what this meant to all of us. May God bless each and every one of you and Grace on Wings organization! Again, thank you so very much for your help Tuesday. You completed her wishes and allowed her to pass peacefully and that means everything in the world to us. If there is ever anything we can do to help out in any possible way please let us know. Thank you from the family of Beckie Galbreath.

A number of my colleagues in Terre Haute saw the television report and praised me for the great work we were doing through Grace on Wings. That made me very uncomfortable. Yes, it was good for people to hear about the ministry and see God at work through us. But I knew God's grace was what enabled us to accomplish anything of value in this life. Remembering Paul's advice to the Philippians, I told them it was a blessing for us to be able to serve people like Beckie during a crisis in life.

16

Abiding In The Vine
("Branching Out, But Not On Your Own")

As I said in the Preface to this book, Grace on Wings is made up of ordinary people doing extraordinary things because God has called us to do so. He equips us with everything we need along this incredible journey.

The ministry began with and continues because of God's calling. We didn't develop a business plan for Grace on Wings and then set about in our own power to make the ministry happen. Instead, we answered the call and followed God's leading. What Pastor Gary Walker said at our first board meeting is still true. "This is just crazy without God being involved."

It took us more than a year from the time Grace on Wings was incorporated to actually have an aircraft to perform the mission we were called to do. Nearly a year and a half went by before we made our first air ambulance flight. Along the way, we incurred a tremendous amount of debt with no earthly guarantee of ever being able to pay any of our bills. As a consequence, we all made sacrifices to accomplish the mission because we knew we were involved in something special, something much larger than ourselves.

By August of 2013, Grace on Wings had served 266 patients and their families during unexpected and life-changing medical crises. We were blessed to see firsthand how God could take ordinary sinners like us and do a miraculous work in spite of our shortcomings. Along the way, we had many opportunities—far more than 266—to share the love of Christ with people who truly needed to feel his presence in their lives.

God continues to challenge our faith.

A New Branch

As more and more people learned about our ministry, the demand for our services continued to grow. Nellie was flying so much she was in the shop for routine maintenance, required by the FAA for all aircraft carrying passengers, approximately two to three months out of the year. During that down time, we still received urgent requests to help patients, but we had no backup aircraft to continue the ministry. We began to pray fervently for God to provide us with a second MU-2 so we could stay operational continuously.

Hal was aware of an MU-2 aircraft parked on the ramp at our maintenance base in Tulsa, Oklahoma. It had been there for two years. He discovered the plane was for sale, and with the board's approval, he made an offer to buy it. Although some maintenance and modifications had to be performed to get the plane ready to function as an air ambulance, our friends at Intercontinental Jet were more than willing to get the new plane ready for us to fly.

Two years before that time, at the AMTC meeting in St. Louis, our friend Ralph Braaten had offered to donate a completely customized, brand new cot system to the Grace on Wings ministry when we had a second aircraft. Ralph had said, "God has blessed me this year in so many ways. I love what you guys are doing, and I want to share my blessings with you."

Hal contacted Ralph and told him of our plans to purchase a second aircraft. Ralph excitedly reaffirmed his offer to donate the $80,000 cot system to Grace on Wings. He then set about making the essential piece of equipment.

Hal's offer for the plane was accepted, and the new MU-2 became a new branch on our growing ministry.

Since Hal had always affectionately referred to Nellie as his "girl," Tami thought it would be appropriate if the new plane could be her "boy." Hal liked the idea and tried to come up with a good male name for the new aircraft. He noticed the tail number for the new plane was N777LP and took the LP to mean the Lord's Promise. So Hal thought the plane should be called Abraham, as God was leading us to a place we could not see but were determined to go because he had told us to do so. Tami liked the idea but recommended we shorten the name to "Abe."

The acquisition of Abe paid immediate dividends for the ministry. We were able to fly five patients using Abe during one time period when Nellie was gone for maintenance.

Blake's Story

Blake C. moved to Tulsa, Oklahoma, from his home in Cookeville, Tennessee, to attend a Bible college and play basketball for the school's team. He had dealt with drug addiction issues for a number of years, but while he was in the last rehab center, Blake rededicated his life to Christ. He remained clean for two years and was feeling optimistic about his life again.

When Blake began his schooling in 2012, however, he was excessively fatigued and short of breath. He passed out one day and was taken to a local doctor. Blood tests were performed, and Blake was told he had critically low levels of red cells, white cells, and platelets in his blood. A bone marrow biopsy was subsequently performed, revealing he had leukemia. He needed to get home to begin chemotherapy. Grace on Wings answered the call.

Blake's family knew he was too sick to fly home on a commercial flight. His father's employer told the family about Grace on Wings. A flight request was made, the usual protocols were followed, and Blake's transport was scheduled.

On the day of transport, our crew found Blake weak, pale, clammy, but in good spirits. Blake's father asked the crew to pray over him before leaving the hospital, and they were happy to oblige. Blake was transported to Vanderbilt University Hospital in Nashville, Tennessee, where he underwent treatment for his disease.

On February 22, 2013, Blake and his family attended the Grace on Wings Gala event. He said his experience with Grace on Wings was so awesome it was hard to put into words. He then went on to give a very passionate testimony as to how God had worked to heal him.

Blake is in remission from leukemia, and he hopes to return to Bible college soon. Who knows what his story will be in the years ahead?

The Twins' Story

Not long ago I received a call from a former member of our church requesting help from Grace on Wings. He told me his granddaughter had come from the state of Washington to visit family and friends in Indiana. She was pregnant with twins and not due to deliver for two months, but she went into labor prematurely. The twins, Peter and Lexie, weighed only three pounds at birth and required a two-month stay in the newborn ICU for treatment of prematurity and respiratory distress. When they were discharged from the hospital, the mother and babies had no way to make the two thousand mile trip home.

Grace on Wings answered the call and transported the twins and their mother to their home in southeastern Washington. What a blessing to be able to serve these children and their family.

Seeing Into The Future

What does the future hold for Grace on Wings? What new shoots will turn into new branches with more fruit? We are hopeful God will continue to bless us so we can expand our operations to reach more people in need. In his perfect timing, we hope to establish a satellite base of operations somewhere in the western part of the U.S. so we can serve more patients in that region of the country.

We frequently receive heart-wrenching requests from patients outside the U.S. who are desperate for help. One mother from Antigua, an island in the Caribbean, recently wrote in an email request, "The transport is for my baby. He is two months old and is in critical condition. He requires ventilation and needs to see a cardiologist to fix a hole in his heart. We are not financially well off and we need your help." Unfortunately, we couldn't help because we do not have an aircraft capable of such a long flight.

Someday we hope to have a jet aircraft that will allow us to serve patients like that two-month-old boy from Antigua. But until then, we will continue answering the call to serve those we can.

Can God use you to serve his people, perhaps even start a new ministry to bring him glory? Absolutely! God is not looking for superheroes. He is looking for ordinary Christians to hear his call to ministry and to be obedient in answering that call.

The Bible gives many examples of how God used ordinary people to accomplish extraordinary things through the power he gave them. Jesus calls the humble John the Baptist the greatest man who ever lived. Chapter 11 of Hebrews is replete with the names of common people who, by faith, followed God's commands and accomplished great things for his kingdom.

When Jesus chose his first disciples, he did not call the most learned and religious men in Israel to be his closest followers. He chose two ordinary fishermen, Peter and Andrew, to be his first followers. From there he called James and John, two more fishermen. Next he added a tax collector, Matthew, to his small group. The other seven men who made up the twelve disciples closest to Jesus were equally as undistinguished as their chosen predecessors.

The key to any success we have had with Grace on Wings is not what we have done, but the extent to which we have understood who we are in relationship to our Creator and his plans. Jesus told his disciples in John 15:5, "I am the vine; you are the branches. If a man remains in me and I in him, he will bear much fruit; apart from me you can do nothing." In addition, he said in John 15:1–2, "My Father is the gardener. He cuts off every branch in me that bears no fruit, while every branch that does bear fruit he prunes so that it will be even more fruitful."

I can envision Jesus walking with his disciples through a vineyard as he took the opportunity to teach them this important principle of the vine. What a marvelous, practical lesson for all of us to consider.

Did you ever think of yourself as a branch? Are you remaining, or abiding, in Jesus? How do you know for sure?

Jesus said we know we are abiding in him if our lives are bearing fruit. What kind of fruit are we called to bear? We, as branches, are to draw love from the vine, which is Jesus, and share that love with others. The apostle Paul wrote in Ephesians 5:1–2, "Be imitators of God, therefore, as dearly loved children and live a life of love, just as Christ loved us and gave himself up for us as a fragrant offering and sacrifice to God."

Jesus gave his life for us so that through his death and resurrection, we who believe in him as the Son of God who was raised from the dead, could have forgiveness of our sins and the promise of eternal life. Now that was love. That was answering the call.

Once we fully grasp the depth of his love, we are compelled by the Holy Spirit to share that love with others. Jesus said even sharing a cup of cold water with someone who is thirsty is a gesture that shows his love. How much more fruit we will bear when we humble ourselves as Christ did and put the interests of others before our own so God can be glorified through us!

Ending Or Just Beginning?

As I was sitting at the computer thinking about how to write a fitting ending for this book, a new request for help from a hospital worker popped up in my Grace on Wings email account. It read, "Would you take a patient from Oahu, Hawaii, to Stanford Hospital in San Jose, California? The patient's insurance will not pay for medical transport, and a heart transplant is needed ASAP. We do not do them here in Hawaii. The patient is forty-seven years old, has eight children, and the youngest child was born this year. Please help!"

It tore me apart to reply, "We can't help you." I then realized this book is not the place and now is not the time to talk about endings. Instead, it is the time to redouble my efforts and by extension, the efforts of Grace on Wings, to show the love of Christ to the world.

I want to be able to answer each call for help with a resounding, "Yes! We will help you." I envision a time when Grace on Wings has bases of operation throughout the world. A time when our ministry possesses jet aircraft that can transport patients from any country on the globe. A time when the love of Christ reaches every region of the world through the ministry God called us to just a few years ago.

We cannot get there on our own. We need you. Come join us in answering the call to serve our neighbors in their time of need. With your help, one day I will have many more stories to tell of how God has used Grace on Wings to serve others.

Testimonials

My patient had been experiencing severe respiratory symptoms. She wanted to see a physician in Chicago to see if there was any hope for her condition. Grace on Wings provided a transport for her to and back from the appointment in Chicago. The Grace on Wings crew cared for her and accompanied her from her home, through the flight, and directly to the doctor's office and back. This transport was one of high risk for the patient due to her complex medical illness. Not only was the care and transport medically excellent, the care was delivered with Christ's love. Thank you for all that you do.

David C. Mares, MD, FCCP
Critical Care/Pulmonary Physician
Medical Director of Critical Care
St. Vincent Anderson Regional Hospital
Anderson, Indiana

My wife and I first met Hal and Tami in 2007. It was then we first learned of their God-inspired dreams of Grace on Wings. Since their early days, we have been involved in supporting their activities through our church and in working various fundraising events. However, I did not become a "regular" volunteer until after my retirement from the FAA in May of 2012. Since that time, I have become a small part of the office staff and perform a sundry of duties in support of this wonderful ministry. I must say, anything I may do pales in comparison to the extraordinary dedication to the ministry that our flight crews and medical crews exhibit each and every day. It truly is a profound and magnificent thing to behold!

I have never in my life been a part of an organization or activity that is so spiritually and personally rewarding. I thank God each and every day for allowing me to become a part of this wonderful mission of outreach to our fellow man and to witness on a daily basis the true goodness of our Lord and Savior Jesus Christ.

Michael Ford
Greenwood, Indiana

Grace on Wings touches my heart. It is such a brave endeavor of Hal and Tami. I can't help but think that it is divinely inspired. I have not been on the flight trips, but my husband Rusty has and tells me about them. I can see how the ministry affects him and how proud he is to volunteer as co-pilot for Hal.

May God bless the whole crew and sponsors of Grace on Wings as they continue to help those critically ill people get home or to another hospital for care. Thank you, thank you.

Cathy Nichols

Our ChristCare Group was in search of a mission project when we were introduced to Hal, the CEO of Grace on Wings. He had a vision of an air ambulance service that would help transport patients, for minimal cost, with the support of volunteers. We were all excited, gathering ideas to get fundraisers started. Today, whenever a flight is accomplished, it feels great knowing we were a part of this mission.

Heidi Marie Ford

I came to Grace On Wings in November 2009 through the leading of the Holy Spirit while I was in the process of completing clinical rotations in pediatrics at Riley Children Hospital in Indianapolis,

Indiana. During that time, my clinical instructor told me about Grace on Wings. Julie told me I needed to be a part of Grace On Wings, and the Lord led in that direction. I wanted to become a flight nurse/paramedic, and I never dreamed I would be able to serve in this capacity through Grace On Wings as I have.

My prayer is for Grace On Wings' ministry to remain steadfast in Jesus Christ. His life, death, and resurrection provide the way for the world to be free of sin and right with God, allowing those who believe in Jesus Christ to have eternal life.

Matt Guy

I knew both Hal and Tami before the ministry of Grace on Wings began. I am a nurse, and Hal and I used to work together in the OR many years ago. Both Hal and Tami are great examples of how we all are called by Christ to serve others and to rely on him for everything.

I have had the privilege and honor of being a small part of this ministry since the first Hog Roast fundraiser, and oh, how God has blessed it. God has used Grace on Wings to impact many lives, including that of my youngest daughter Chelsea. She is currently in nursing school and works closely with Hal and Tami, who have been such a blessing and inspiration to her. She absolutely loves spending time with them and is looking forward to volunteering full-time when she finishes her degree.

Grace on Wings has been a blessing to me in several ways. First, by how it has brought so many volunteers together from many different walks of life. I see the pure joy they receive as they serve alongside one another. Second, God has used Grace on Wings to bless so many families across the nation that otherwise would not have been helped. Third, seeing so many people grow in their faith and seeking God's will in their lives is a blessing as well. Finally, it has been a blessing to our entire family by allowing us to serve together.

May God continue to richly bless this ministry.

Jimmy, Shelli, and Chelsea Engle

Grace on Wings allows me the opportunity to minister to people in a holistic, mind-body-spirit manner, unencumbered by outside agendas, truly doing God's work. This ministry proves to be very satisfying work on a soul level.

JoLynne Anderson, BSN, RN

Grace on Wings has brought such blessing in my life. I started doing volunteer aircraft cleaning work on Nellie a few years ago, shortly after starting the Grace on Wings Bible study at the home base in Indy sometime in 2010. In January of 2013, I lost my biggest cleaning contract and didn't know what I was going to do. Hal offered me the job of cleaning Nellie once a month, and that gave me hope that I would be okay. I also got an office cleaning contract with one of the airport facilities. It was hard for me to keep a dry eye while writing this piece. May God continue to bless Grace on Wings.

Christine Zimmerman

This past year being a part of Grace on Wings has not only allowed me to meet new friends but also to grow my faith in the Lord. I have been on multiple flights, and my faith has grown to a point that I pray with all my patients. Through this ministry I have been blessed with lifelong friends, including other volunteers and patients. I praise God everyday for this ministry, and I'm very grateful to be a small part that it takes to help so many lives.

Dannielle Hunnicutt, NREMT-P

God has afforded me countless "God Moments" with opportunity to serve and minister during my volunteer activities with Grace on Wings. When I shared about the ministry to a young woman named Elizabeth, she picked Grace on Wings as her Girl Scout community service project. She and her family made huggable pillows in the shape of a cross for Grace on Wings patients. The family and I also came up with last year's design for the Grace on Wings calendar.

I have the privilege of writing stories for the Grace on Wings newsletter. I have a camera that is always with me, and when Grace on Wings cannot find a professional photographer, they call on me. You never know what God is willing to bring to you when you are simply willing to serve.

G. Polly Jordan

I met Tami while we were both working in the ER at St. Clare Hospital in Crawfordsville. She shared with me details about Grace on Wings and its Christian mission. I was very interested in what they were doing, and I had lots of questions; this seemed like the mission field for me.

After becoming a GOW volunteer, I was very moved by Hal and Tami's dedication to their mission and their unselfish trust in the Lord. Handing everything over to God has been difficult for me, but seeing the Blank's complete trust in the Lord and the blessings they have received has helped me grow as a Christian.

Todd Fouty, Paramedic/Firefighter
Crawfordsville Fire Department

After attending a couple of fundraiser dinners and volunteering at the annual Hog Roast, I can understand the praise for the great work Grace on Wings does. When I think of the people I've met because of this ministry, I smile.

Linnie Fullenkamp

As I think about how Grace on Wings is a service unto our Lord and what my testimony about it is, I think of home. It's a place where we can be surrounded by loved ones, a place where we can feel secure and cared for, a place of comfort at the end of the day.

I think of the smiles on patients' faces when our team arrived. They were going home! Some had been in a strange land, away from their families, sick and injured, discouraged and worried. But through the service of Grace on Wings and by the grace of our Lord, they were going home.

I feel so privileged to have been a small part of Grace on Wings in this service to our Lord and Savior.

Patti

Hal Blank, CEO and Chief Pilot, has always said that Grace on Wings began on a "wing and a prayer," but without the solid team built to begin this ministry, their ability to see it grow and prosper would not have been possible. Initially, in the eyes of a bank, this was another start-up company. We liked their idea, but it was their sound business plan and realistic projections that gave The Farmers Bank the confidence to get involved.

Overall this has been a great relationship with a very well run company. We were excited for them when Nellie, their first air ambulance got her new engines, and Abe, the most recent aircraft was added to the fleet. I have become passionate about their mission and support them not only as their loan officer but personally as well. I look forward to our ongoing relationship as we continue to do our small part in their very large mission of "showing God's love through aviation."

Thanks for the opportunity to express why the bank believes in Grace on Wings.

Kendra Price
Commercial Loan Officer at The Farmers Bank

Notes

Chapter 3

Page 46: "Al told me his crew …": Wayne Thompson, *To Hanoi And Back*. Washington, D.C. : Smithsonian Institution Press, 2000, page 274.

Chapter 4

Page 50: "A quote from a nineteenth-century …": John Piper, "Is Anything Too Hard For God?" Audio sermon on October 18, 1987. www.desiringgod.org/resource-library/sermons/is-anything-too-hard-for-god.

Chapter 5

Page 64: "In considering the major …": Henry Blackaby, *Experiencing God (Revised and Expanded)*. Nashville, Tennessee: Life Way Press, 1990, page 21.

Chapter 6

Page 68: "Charles Spurgeon, the influential …": C.H. Spurgeon, "Is Anything Too Hard For The Lord?" Sermon #2020. London, England: 1888. www.spurgeongems.org, page 8.

Chapter 8

Page 92: "About ten years ago ...": Randy Alcorn, *The Treasure Principle*. Sisters, Oregon: Multnomah Publishers, 2001, pages 6–16.

Page 93: "John Piper points out ...": John Piper, "Getting Old for the Glory of God." Audio sermon on September 30, 2007. www.desiringgod.org/resource-library/sermons/getting-old-for-the-glory-of-god.

About The Author

James R. Milstead, an emergency medicine physician, is the Medical Director for Grace on Wings. In addition to his work with Grace on Wings, he has been involved in short-term Christian mission work around the world for more than twenty years. He lives with his wife, Becky, in Frankfort, Indiana. He and his wife have three children and seven grandchildren.

CPSIA information can be obtained at www.ICGtesting.com
Printed in the USA
LVOW05s0252131213

365025LV00003B/5/P